LEADERSHIP

In Action

Inspiration for
Intentional Leadership

LYNNE ROE

Copyright © 2022 by Lynne Roe

All rights reserved. No part of this book may be reproduced in any form or by any electronic or mechanical means including information storage and retrieval systems, without permission in writing from the publisher. The only exception is by a reviewer, who may quote short excerpts in a review. For permission requests, please address The Three Tomatoes Publishing.

Published October 2022
ISBN: 979-8-9871051-3-9

For information address:
The Three Tomatoes Book Publishing
6 Soundview Rd.
Glen Cove, NY 11542
www.thethreetomatoespublishing.com

Cover design: Tony Iatridis
Interior design: Tony Iatridis

All company and/or product names may be trade names, logos, trademarks, and/or registered trademarks and are the property of their respective owners.

The Three Tomatoes Book Publishing

*This book is dedicated to those leaders
who want to live life with intention and
consciously strive to leave the world
a little better than they found it.*

CONTENTS

Forward 1
Action/Change 3
Influence/Connection 13
Learning/Growth 23
Contribution/Service 33
Creativity/Innovation 43
Collaboration/Teamwork 53
Positivity/Possibility 63
Intention/Commitment 73
Preparation/Planning 83
Consistency 91
Passion/Purpose 101
Enthusiasm and Inspiration 111
About the Author 120

FORWARD

I believe that everyone has an opportunity to lead at different times in their life. And I believe that everyone has opportunities to lead regardless of the title that they have. Even as a solopreneur you have an opportunity to lead with your clients or customers, and you may be building a support team of contractors. The concepts in this book can apply to anyone. My favorite definition of leadership comes from Kevin Cashman.

> **Leadership is courageous, authentic influence that creates enduring value.**
> ~ *Kevin Cashman*

After years of working with managers, executives, and business owners in for-profit and not-for-profit organizations, I have seen how leading with intention leads to success. However, in today's world, it's all too easy to lose focus and get pulled off track.

Words of wisdom have a way of helping us reframe our thinking and channel it in productive directions. I have gathered these quotes from my weekly blogs – along with the commentary about them – to invite leaders to pause. Step back from what distracts them. And refocus on what matters most in leading themselves and others.

The quotes are organized into 12 areas of leadership. You can find inspiration by selecting a relevant chapter or simply opening the book to any page. Resist the urge to take a quick glance and move on with your day. I've found that the more time you invest in thinking about these ideas, the more value you get from them.

The commentary that accompanies each quote offers suggestions for putting thought into action. Look for ways to be intentional day in and day out. Start with a new action just once or for a week, then extend it to a month, a year, or more. Your success will come from regular practices that keep you moving forward.

My heartfelt thanks to the authors, historical figures, colleagues, and clients who have asked questions, shared ideas, and shown me examples. They've enriched my life, shaped my thinking, and helped me along my path and I hope they will help you as well.

~ *Lynne*

Leadership In Action

ACTION/CHANGE

Leadership In Action

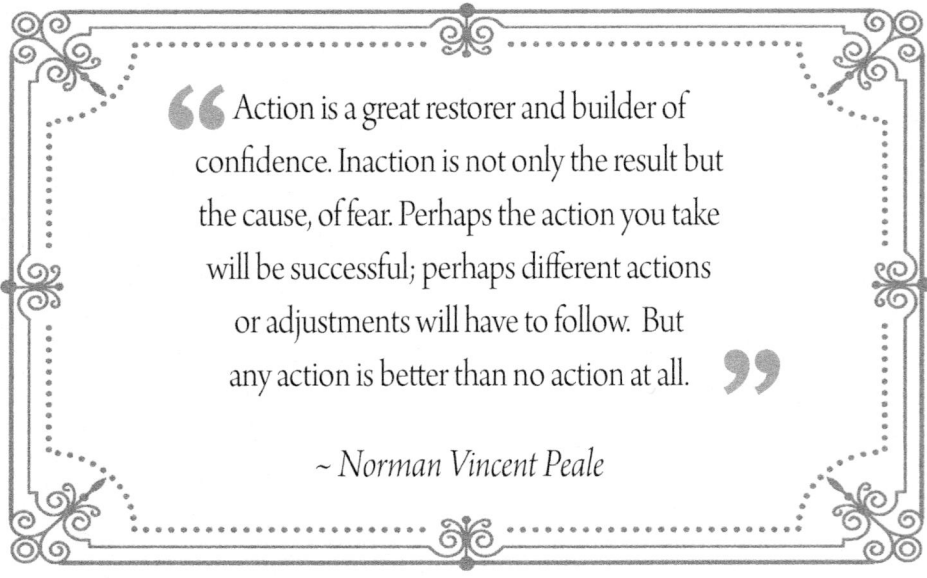

> "Action is a great restorer and builder of confidence. Inaction is not only the result but the cause, of fear. Perhaps the action you take will be successful; perhaps different actions or adjustments will have to follow. But any action is better than no action at all."
>
> ~ Norman Vincent Peale

Taking action is necessary for all growth or change. What initiative do you feel is not moving forward as you had hoped? As a leader, how can you take action or encourage your team to take action? What might happen if you just get started?

Action/Change

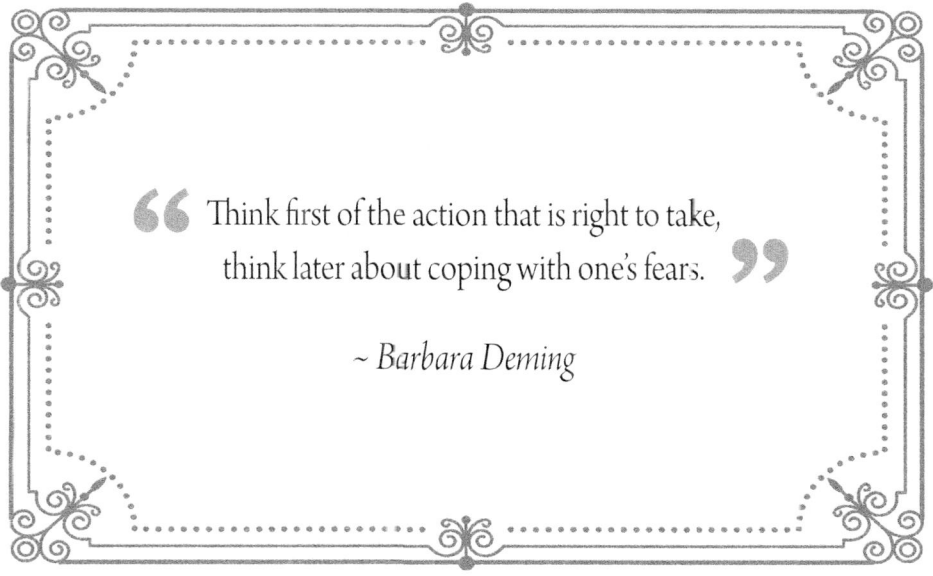

" Think first of the action that is right to take, think later about coping with one's fears. "

~ Barbara Deming

Often people don't take initiative or action towards their goals because of fear, fear of the unknown, fear of what might happen, or fear of what might not happen. But inaction will never get you to your goals. As a leader, you must keep your team in action toward the organization's goals. How can you get your team to put aside their fears and take one beginning action this week?

Leadership In Action

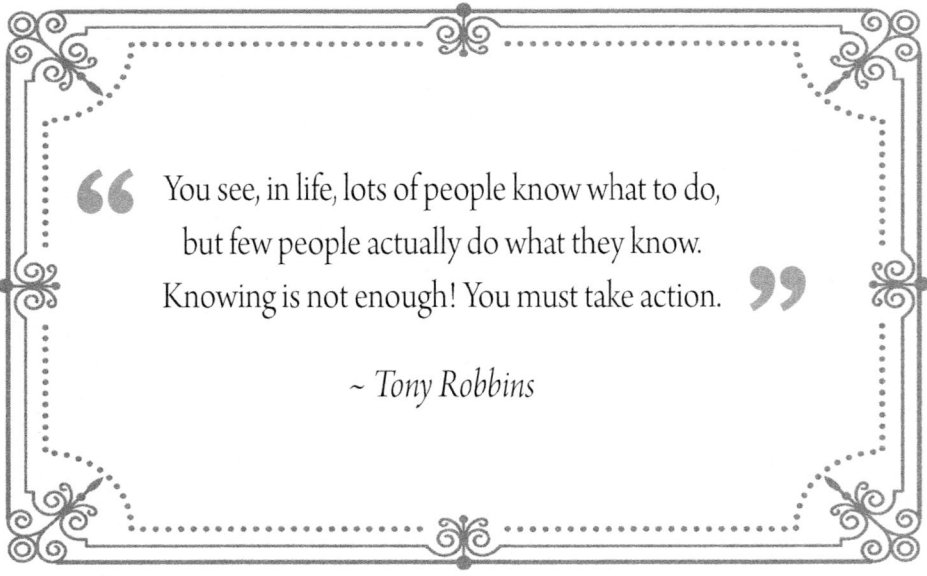

> "You see, in life, lots of people know what to do, but few people actually do what they know. Knowing is not enough! You must take action."
>
> ~ *Tony Robbins*

Where have you been postponing action in your life or your work even though you know what you should do? Think of the first small action step you can take towards that goal. Take that first small step today. The rest will follow more easily.

Action/Change

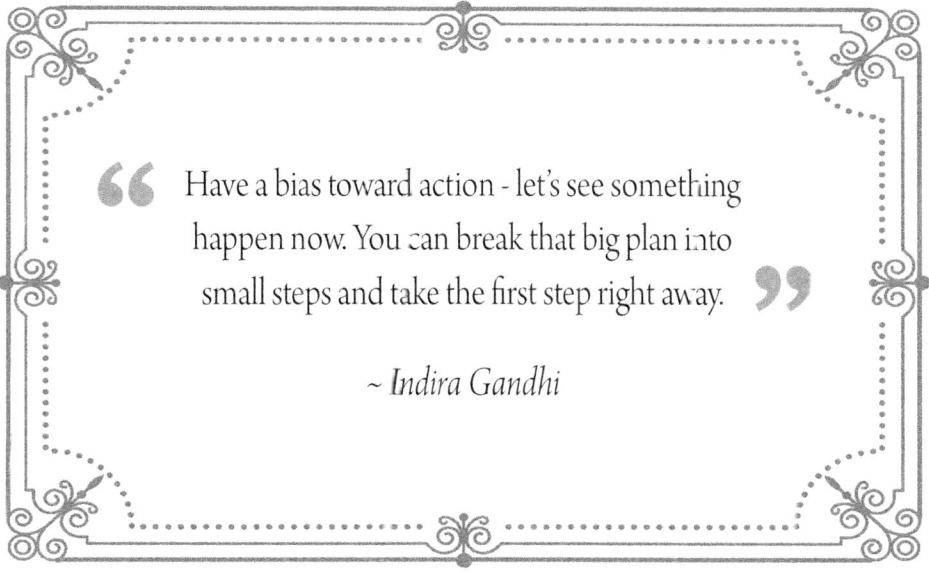

> Have a bias toward action - let's see something happen now. You can break that big plan into small steps and take the first step right away.
>
> ~ Indira Gandhi

As a leader, you must influence those around you to take action towards a specified outcome. Breaking the action down into smaller steps makes it easier to get started. Encourage a bias toward action.

Leadership In Action

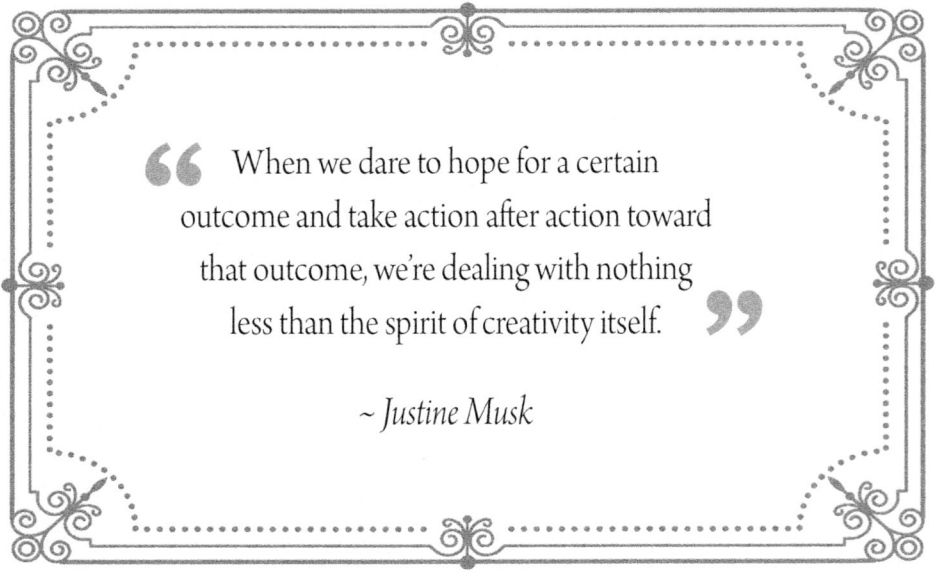

> " When we dare to hope for a certain outcome and take action after action toward that outcome, we're dealing with nothing less than the spirit of creativity itself. "
>
> ~ *Justine Musk*

What is the outcome of taking consistent action towards a specific goal? Consider how you will feel a year from now if you don't take consistent action. When the progress towards your goals gets difficult how can you use your creativity to continue taking steps towards the outcome you seek?

Action/Change

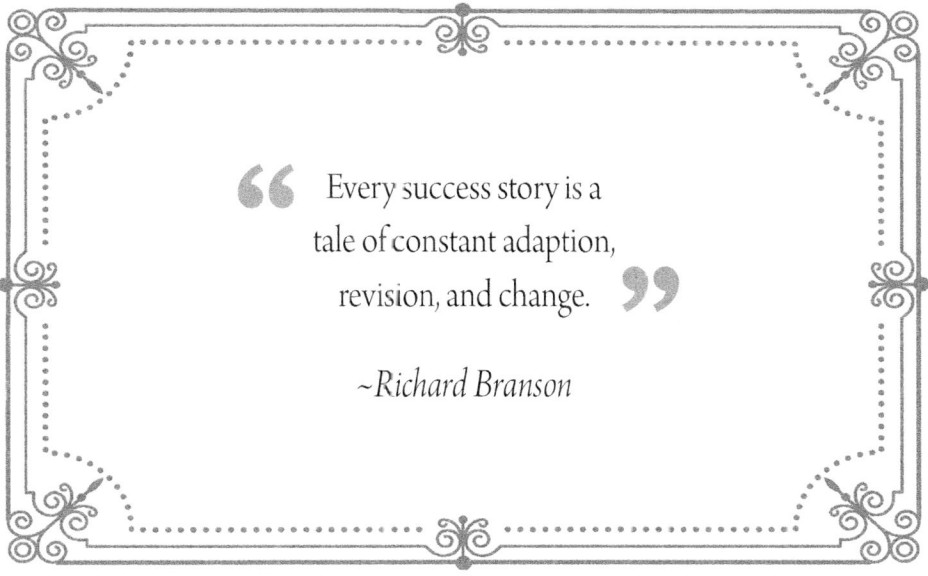

> " Every success story is a tale of constant adaption, revision, and change. "
>
> ~Richard Branson

The world doesn't stop - it is constantly changing. For us to be successful, we must also change and adapt. Generally, the organization that adapts the best quickly, is the most successful.

Leadership In Action

> " To improve is to change; to be perfect is to change often. "
>
> ~ *Winston Churchill*

Don't be afraid to change often. This is one of the fastest ways to improve. Try something, learn from the experience, then try something else.

Action/Change

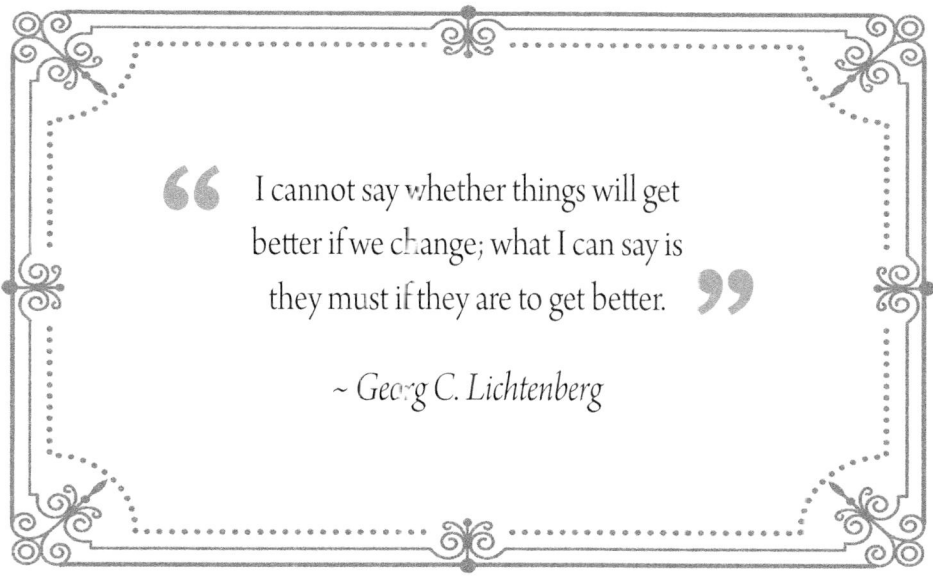

> " I cannot say whether things will get better if we change; what I can say is they must if they are to get better. "
>
> ~ Georg C. Lichtenberg

Often, you can't know that the changes you are making will make things better, but if you continue doing what you have been doing, you will get the same results. What can you change this week to test if it will make things better?

Leadership In Action

INFLUENCE/CONNECTION

Leadership In Action

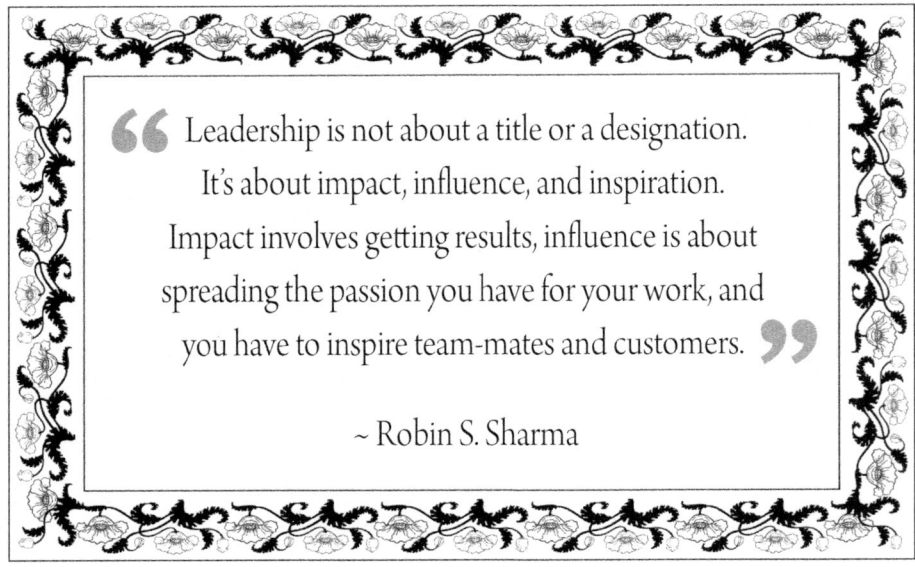

> " Leadership is not about a title or a designation. It's about impact, influence, and inspiration. Impact involves getting results, influence is about spreading the passion you have for your work, and you have to inspire team-mates and customers. "
>
> ~ Robin S. Sharma

Using Robin Sharma's definition of leadership, it is clear how you can be a leader at any position in an organization. How are you leading in your organization, with those above you and those below you or with your customers? Where can you spread your passion and inspire others? Take some time this week to influence someone on your team by communicating your passion and inspiring them too.

Influence/Connection

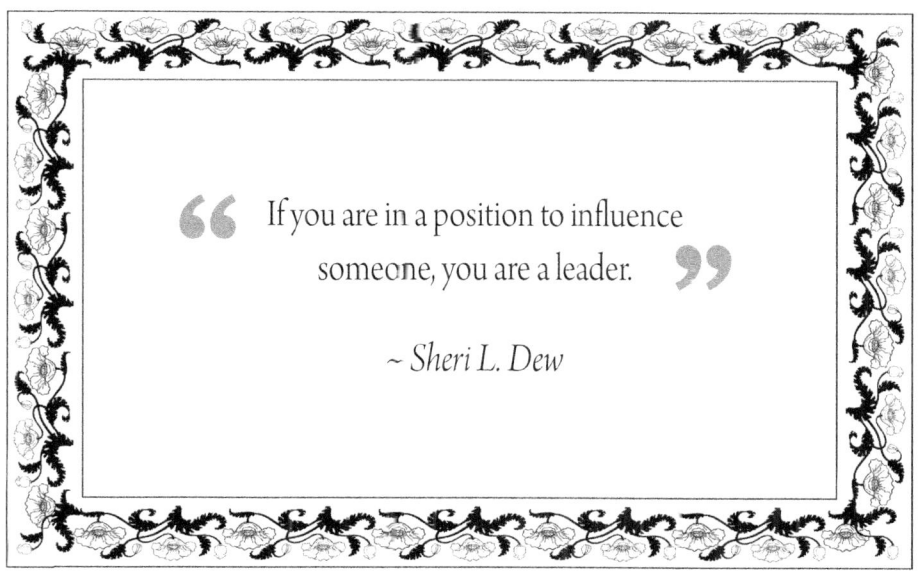

> " If you are in a position to influence someone, you are a leader. "
>
> ~ *Sheri L. Dew*

Leadership is about influence. Where are you in a position to have influence? Consider how you chose to lead in that situation regardless of your title.

Leadership In Action

> " To listen well is as powerful
> a means of communication
> and influence as to talk well. "
>
> ~ *John Marshall*

We don't often think about how we could influence others without talking and spreading our point of view. Leadership is a way of being – so when you listen with the intent to fully understand the speaker and their point of view, you are creating influence. Try it this week - have one conversation where you listen deeply for true understanding and see what effect it might have on your future interactions.

Influence/Connection

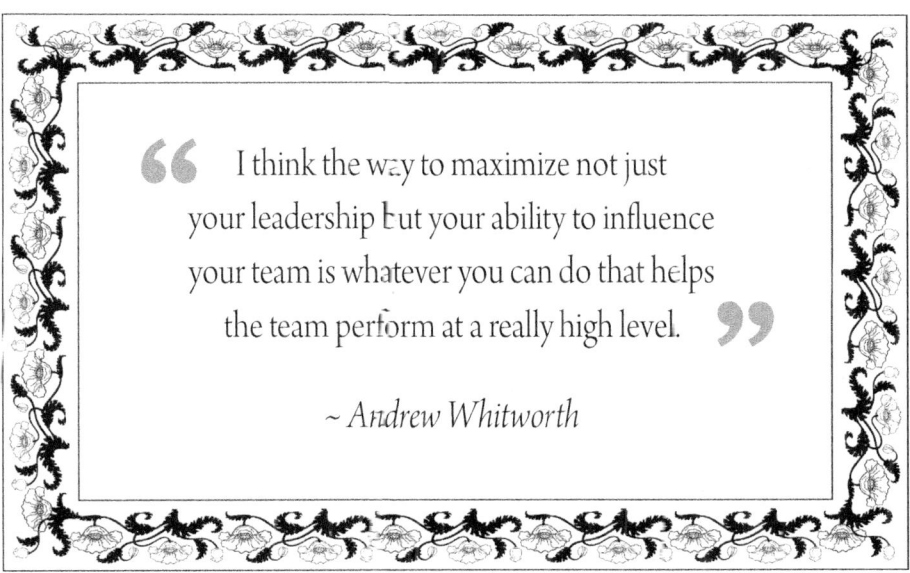

> " I think the way to maximize not just your leadership but your ability to influence your team is whatever you can do that helps the team perform at a really high level. "
>
> ~ Andrew Whitworth

Leadership is about supporting each member of your team so that they can do their work to the best of their ability. When you support the team and everyone is doing their very best, you have the greatest influence on the outcomes. What is one thing you can do this week to support someone on your team to perform at their very best?

Leadership In Action

> " I define connection as the energy that exists between people when they feel seen, heard, and valued; when they can give and receive without judgment; and when they derive sustenance and strength from the relationship. "
>
> ~ Brené Brown

 Leaders are constantly looking for ways to build connections with others. This week, pay attention to how you are building connection energy by making sure that someone feels seen, heard, and valued.

Influence/Connection

> "At their core, an influencer creates an empowering human connection."
>
> ~ Angela Ahrendts

Leaders know that to influence others, you must first develop an empowering connection with them. What can you do this week to further your connection with someone?

Leadership In Action

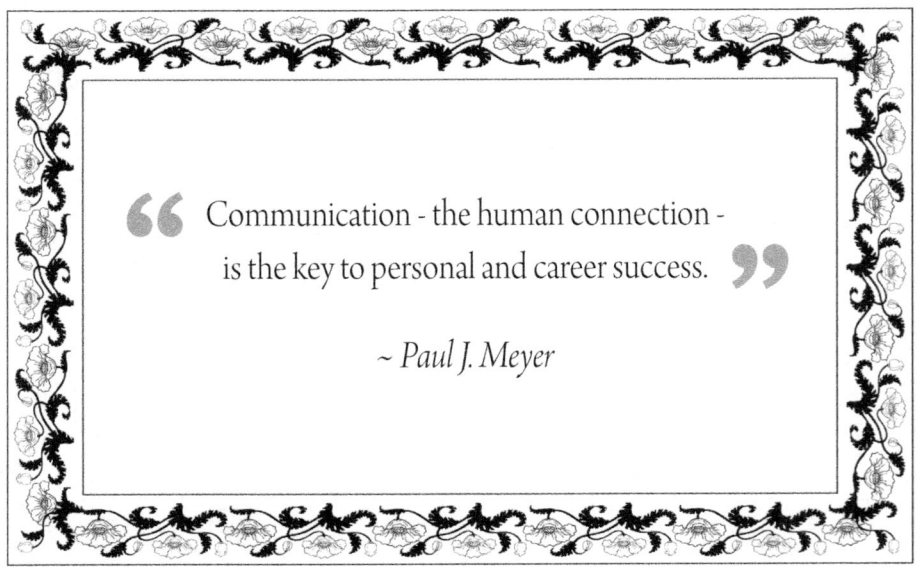

> " Communication - the human connection - is the key to personal and career success. "
>
> ~ *Paul J. Meyer*

We know that communication is how we build connections with others, but we often get caught up in our projects and forget to focus on building those connections. Before you begin work on a project this week, think about who you need to build a connection with to make the project outstanding.

Influence/Connection

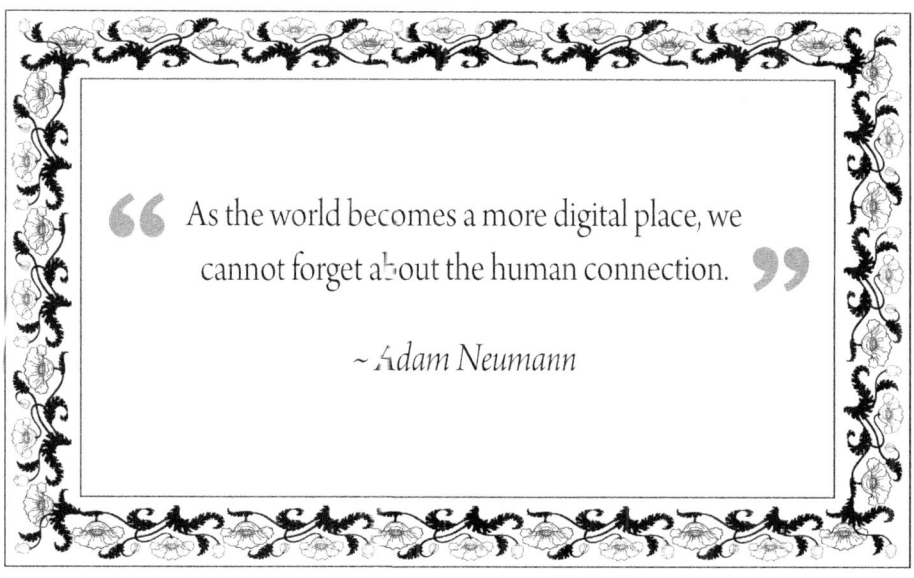

It is so easy to get caught up in our digital world, but personal interaction is a quicker and stronger way to connect.
Take some time this week to connect with someone in person.

> "When people do things they weren't even sure they were capable of, I think it comes back to connection. Connection with teammates. Connection with organization. Feeling like they belong in the environment. I think it's a human need - the need to feel connected."
>
> ~ *Theo Epstein*

 Building connections with your business team is one of the most important roles of a leader. When your team members feel connected to and supported by you and others, they are able to stretch and grow and learn new things - becoming even more valuable to the team.

LEARNING/GROWTH

Leadership In Action

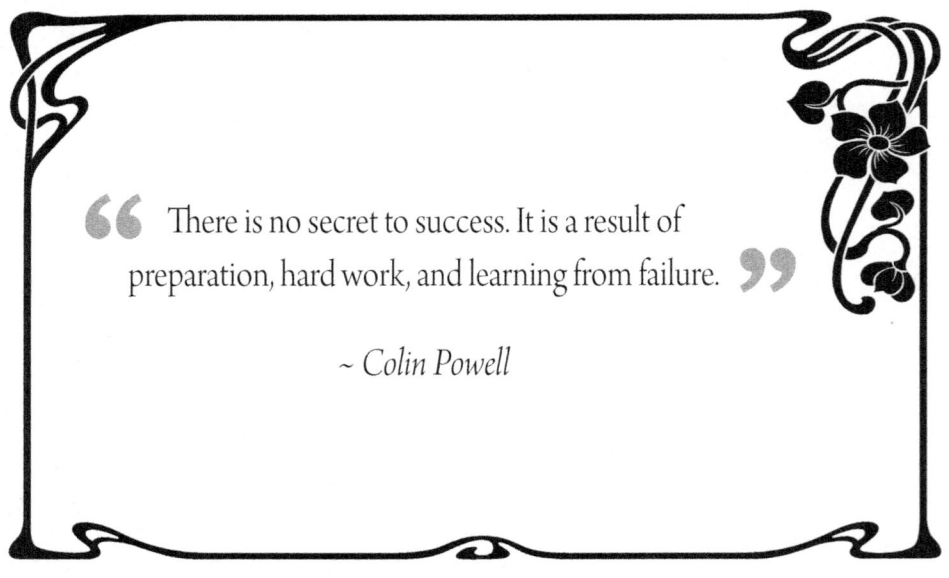

> There is no secret to success. It is a result of preparation, hard work, and learning from failure.
>
> ~ Colin Powell

It is never easy to fail, but as leaders, we need to focus ourselves and our team on learning from each disappointment. Where can you refocus your attention on learning this week?

Learning/Growth

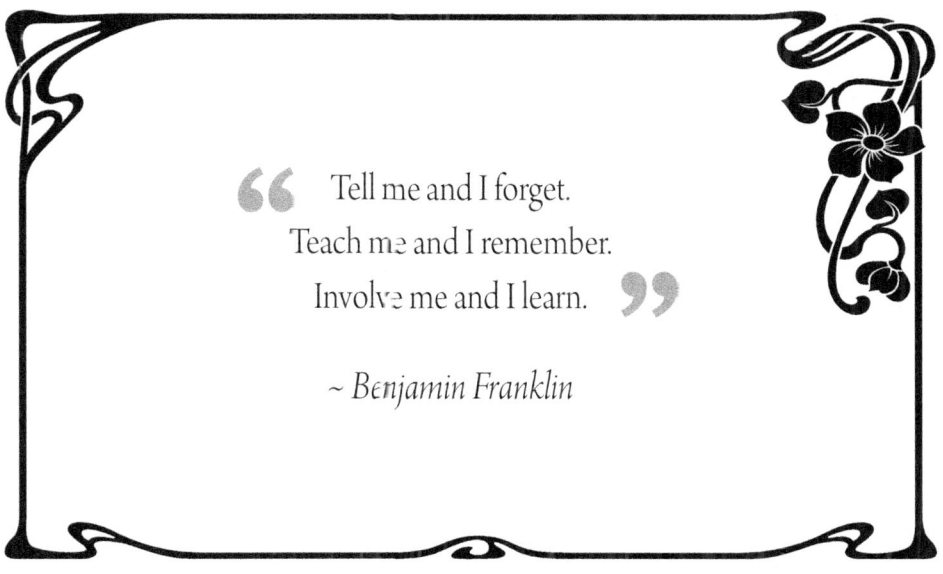

> " Tell me and I forget.
> Teach me and I remember.
> Involve me and I learn. "
>
> ~ Benjamin Franklin

We have a tendency to just show someone how to do something and assume that they have learned it.
As leaders, we need to do more than that by involving our team in the process and allowing them to learn from their mistakes and successes.

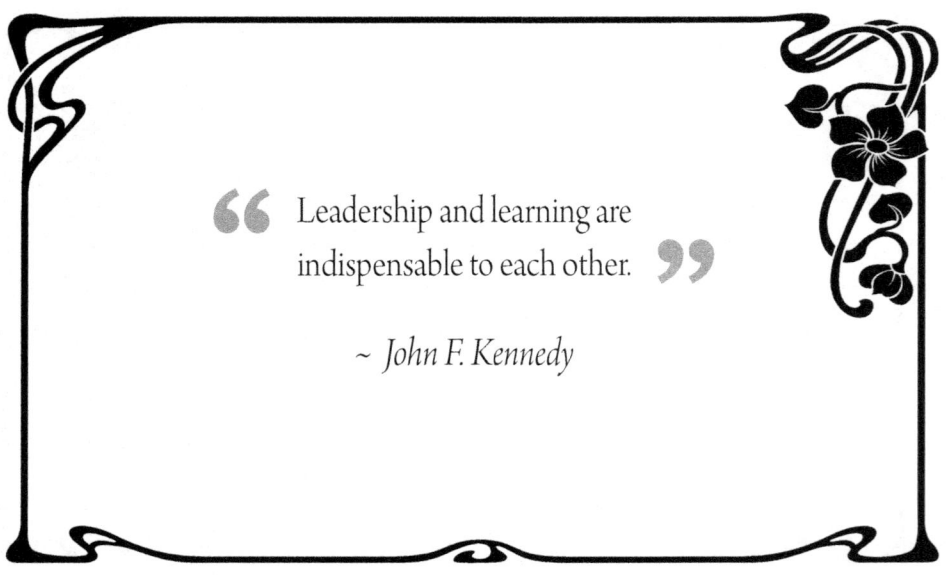

As a leader, it is important to dedicate yourself to learning. You can learn from your successes, your failures, or from others. You can learn about leadership, your industry, your products, your people, yourself, etc. There is always something you can learn in every situation and you never know when that knowledge will help you make better decisions.

Learning/Growth

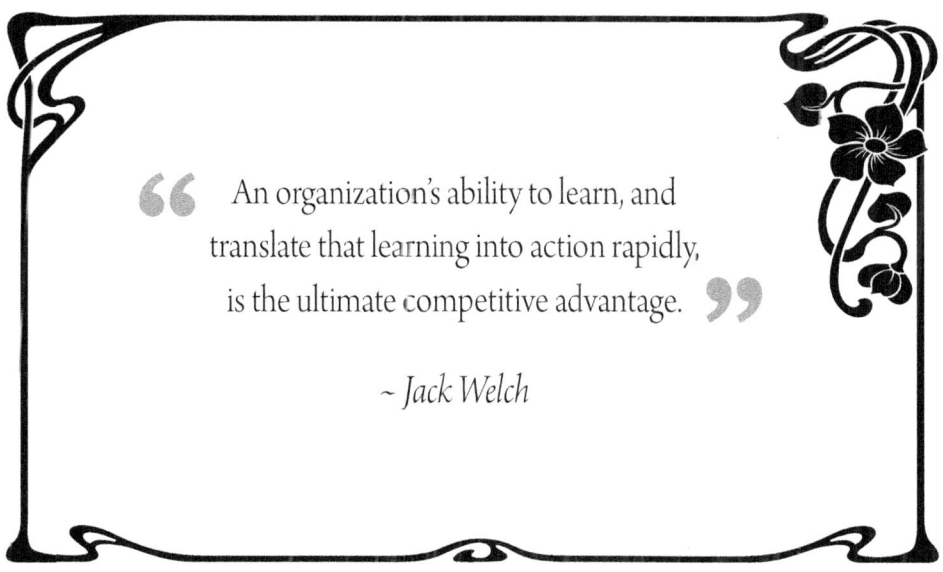

> "An organization's ability to learn, and translate that learning into action rapidly, is the ultimate competitive advantage."
>
> ~ Jack Welch

It is not enough to just learn something, to make progress you need to translate that learning into action. What 0learning can you act on this week that will become your competitive advantage?

Leadership In Action

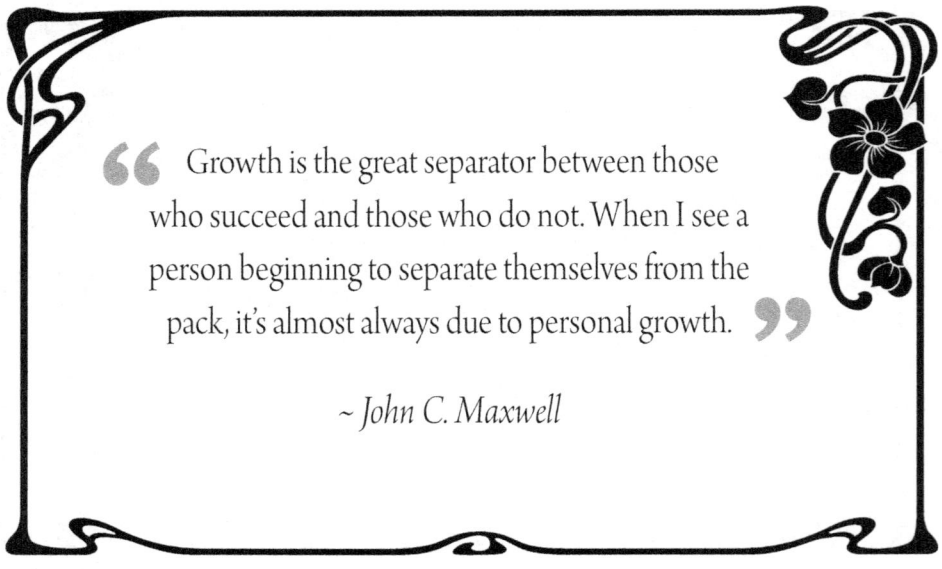

> Growth is the great separator between those who succeed and those who do not. When I see a person beginning to separate themselves from the pack, it's almost always due to personal growth.
>
> ~ *John C. Maxwell*

As leaders, we often want to help our team members grow, and we need to pay attention to our growth as well. What is an area where you would like to grow personally? Choose one area today and take some small action to get you started. How might your personal growth impact your interaction with your team?

Learning/Growth

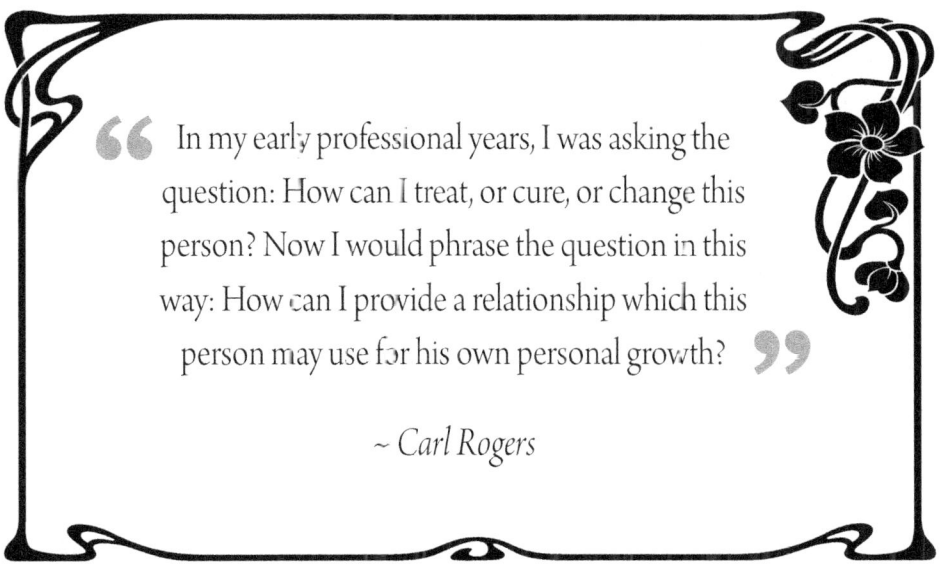

> In my early professional years, I was asking the question: How can I treat, or cure, or change this person? Now I would phrase the question in this way: How can I provide a relationship which this person may use for his own personal growth?
>
> ~ Carl Rogers

Leadership happens when you develop relationships with your team and can influence them. What is your relationship with your team? How can you show up in that relationship to support the growth of your team members?

Leadership In Action

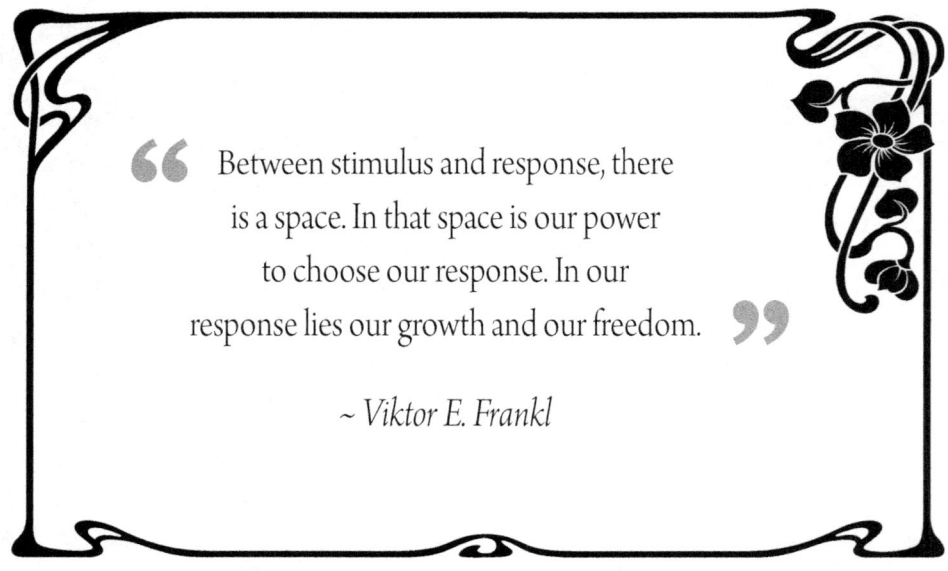

> " Between stimulus and response, there is a space. In that space is our power to choose our response. In our response lies our growth and our freedom. "
>
> ~ *Viktor E. Frankl*

Take some time to pause and recognize something you learned today. In that pause, the lessons of our life become recognized and available for our growth.

Learning/Growth

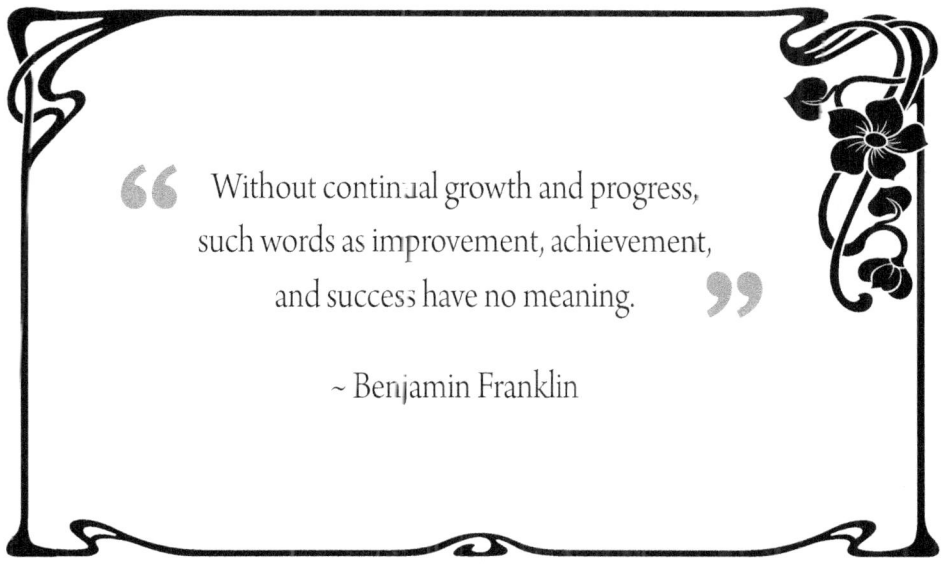

> " Without continual growth and progress, such words as improvement, achievement, and success have no meaning. "
>
> ~ Benjamin Franklin

Do you have a continuous process to expand your growth and learning both personally and for your team? Continuous growth not only leads your business to improvement, achievement, and success, it also helps to keep your team stimulated and engaged in their work. Ask the members of your team this week, in what areas they would like to grow - then help them make it happen!

Leadership In Action

CONTRIBUTION/SERVICE

Leadership In Action

> " Each of us is a unique strand in
> the intricate web of life and
> here to make a contribution. "
>
> ~ *Deepak Chopra*

 We all have the opportunity to contribute throughout our lives, each of us is unique. What is the contribution you can make this week that will support someone else?

Contribution/Service

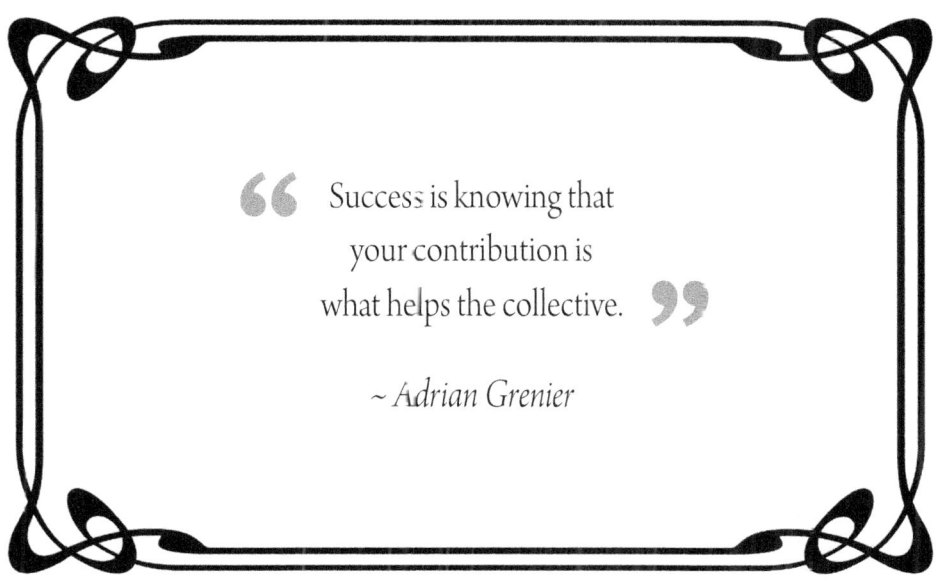

> " Success is knowing that your contribution is what helps the collective. "
>
> ~ Adrian Grenier

Leaders know that their focus needs to be on how their efforts support the individuals they are working with. Who are you supporting this week and how is your contribution making a difference? How does that effort contribute to success?

Leadership In Action

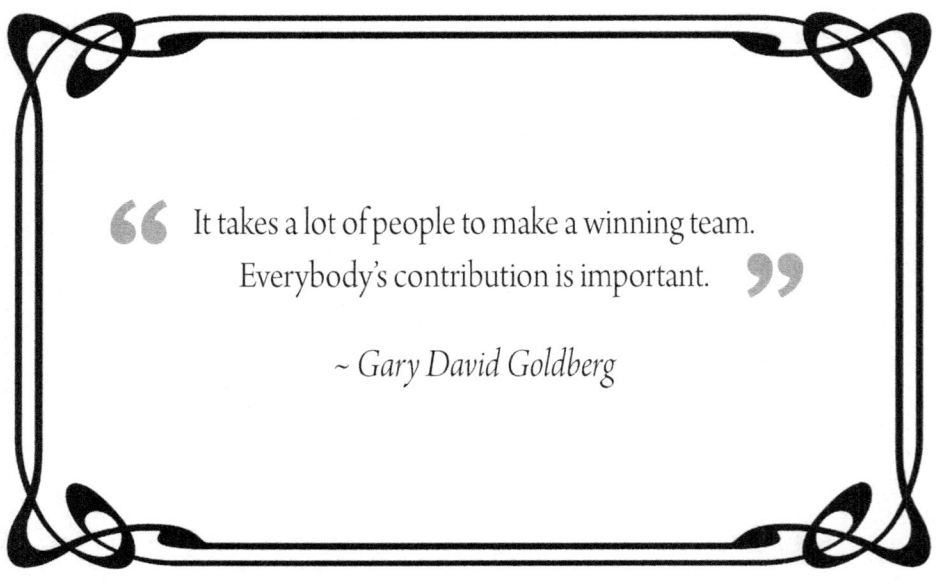

> " It takes a lot of people to make a winning team. Everybody's contribution is important. "
>
> ~ *Gary David Goldberg*

Leaders make an effort to recognize and acknowledge the contributions of each of the team members. Who do you need to recognize this week? Let them know that you recognize and appreciate their contribution.

Contribution/Service

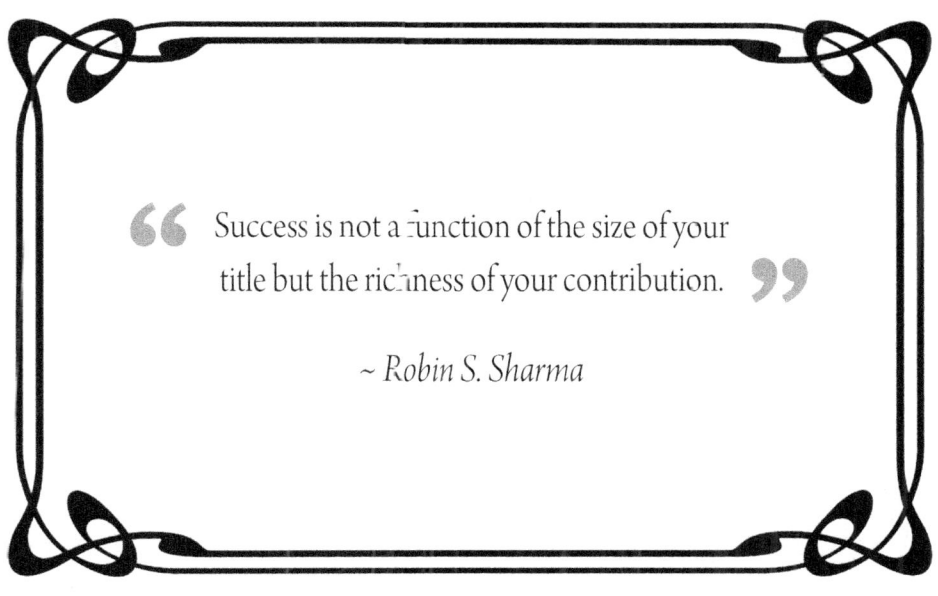

> " Success is not a function of the size of your title but the richness of your contribution. "
>
> ~ Robin S. Sharma

What contribution are you making to the world this week? How can you have an even bigger impact?

Leadership In Action

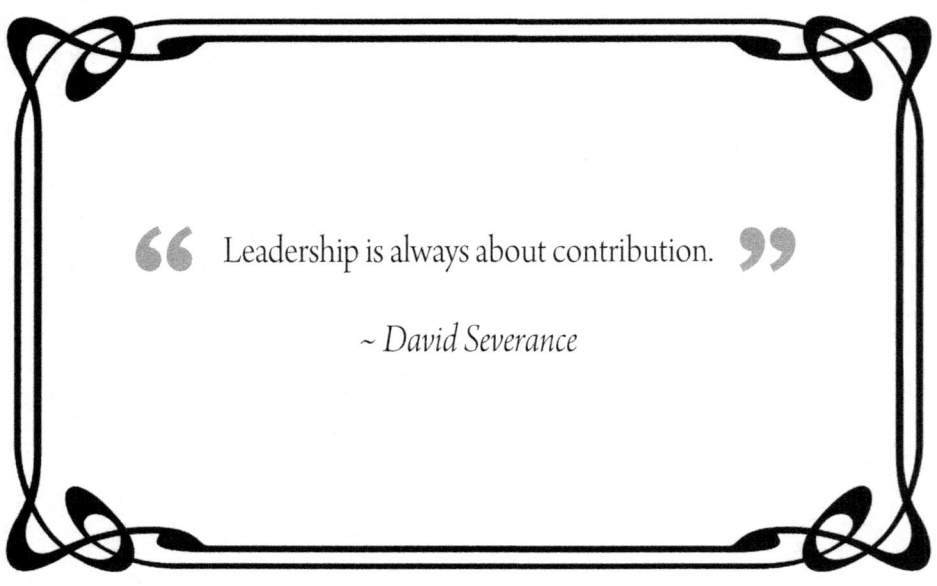

> " Leadership is always about contribution. "
>
> *~ David Severance*

Everything we do as a leader is to support our team and our organization. It is all about the contribution we provide. Ask yourself this week, how do my efforts this week contribute to the success of my team or my organization?

Contribution/Service

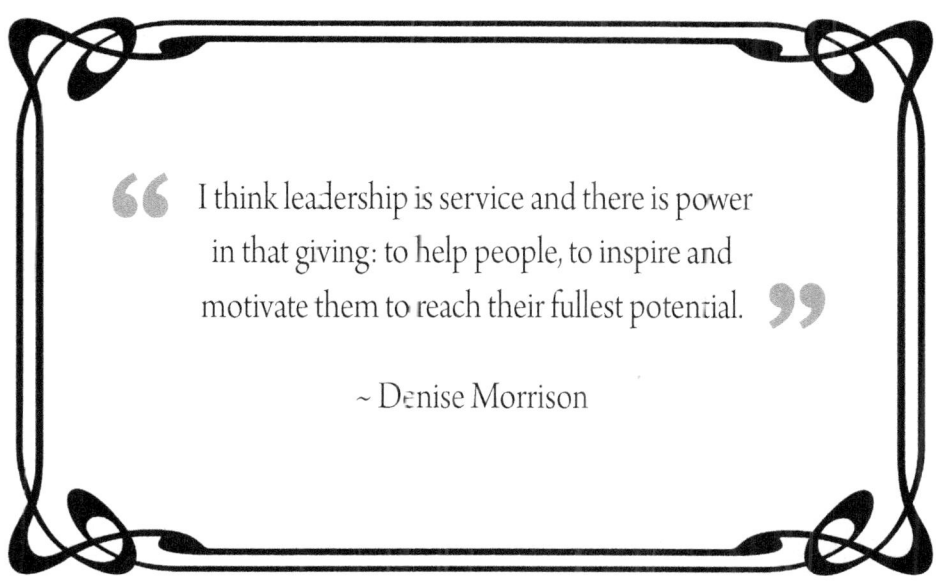

> I think leadership is service and there is power in that giving: to help people, to inspire and motivate them to reach their fullest potential.
>
> ~ Denise Morrison

How do you think about your leadership? A great leader helps their team and motivates them. Consider your interactions this week with your team. What can you do to help them reach their potential?

Leadership In Action

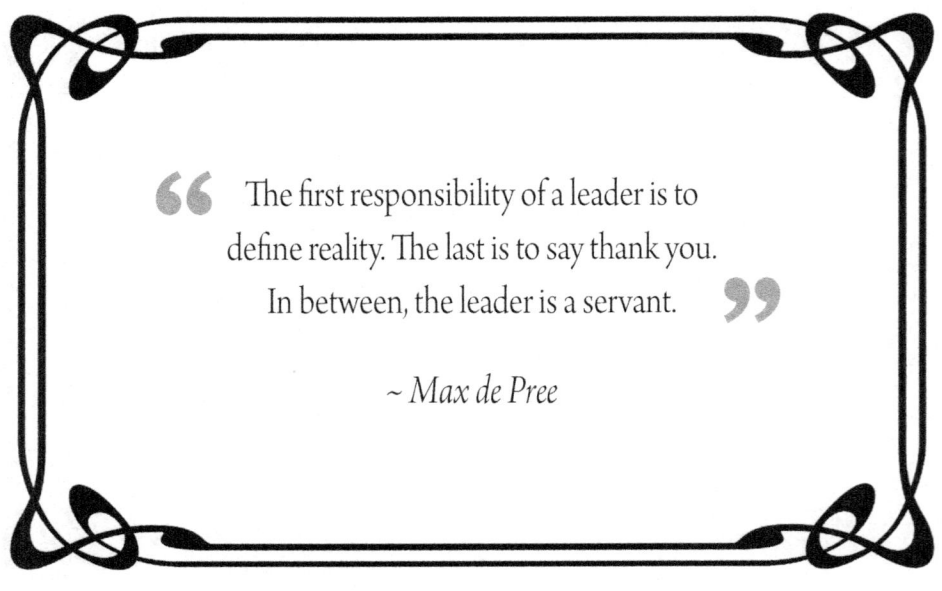

> " The first responsibility of a leader is to define reality. The last is to say thank you. In between, the leader is a servant. "
>
> ~ *Max de Pree*

How clearly have you defined reality for your team? Does your team know the expected outcome of the work you are doing? Once everyone is going in the same direction, how can you support them to do their job excellently? A great leader clearly defines the direction you are going, supports the team to reach that goal, and says thank you along the way, as well as at the end.

Contribution/Service

> " One of the topics I'm most passionate about is servant leadership - the greatest leaders recognize that they're here to serve, not to be served. "
>
> ~ Ken Blanchard

What can I do this week to support a team member? What does the team member need to succeed? These are questions that great leaders ask themselves all the time. What could happen if you asked yourself these questions every week?

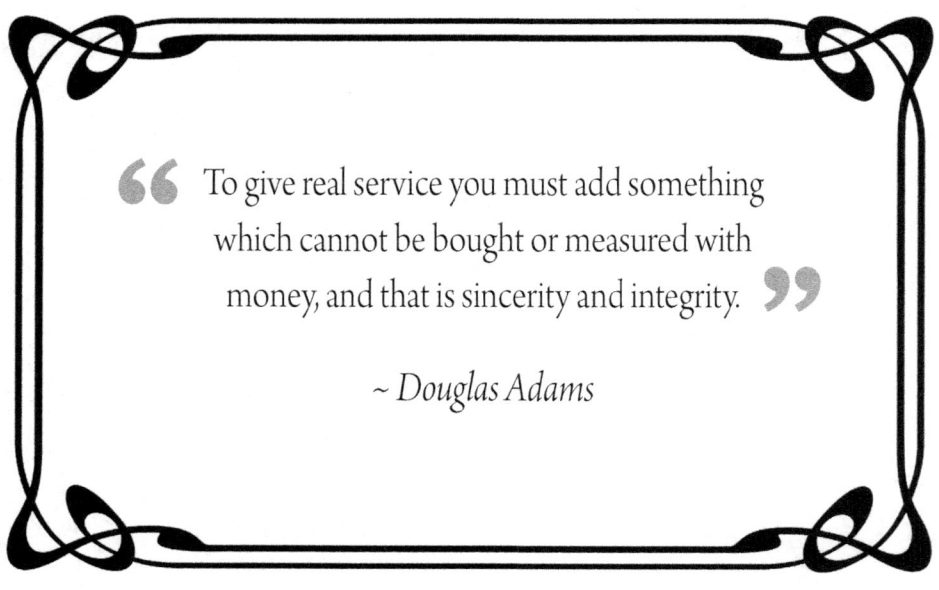

> "To give real service you must add something which cannot be bought or measured with money, and that is sincerity and integrity."
>
> *~ Douglas Adams*

Great leaders recognize the importance of being sincere and true to their word, whether that is with a client/customer or with their team. How well do you follow through on your word? Think carefully this week about how you can ensure that you keep your word.

CREATIVITY/INNOVATION

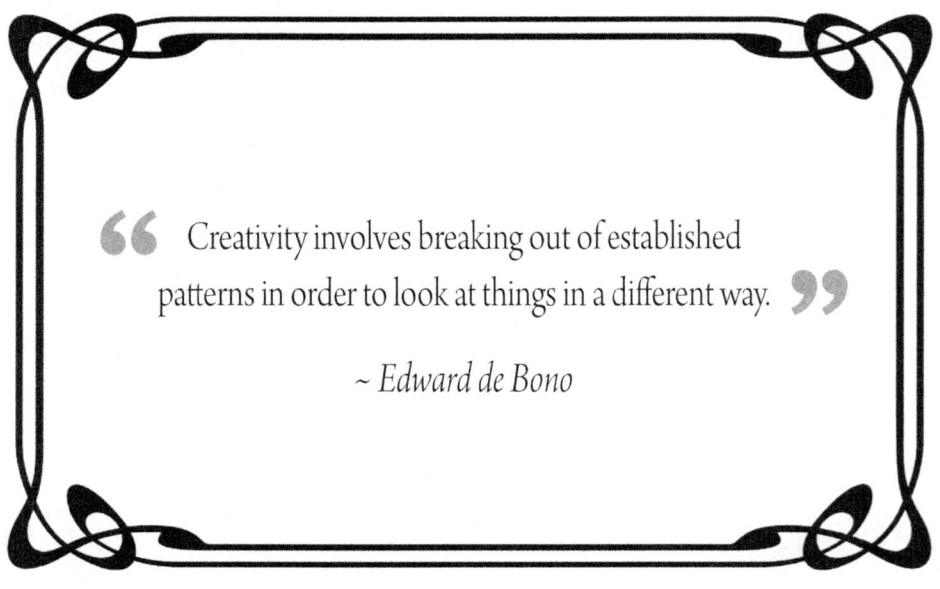

> Creativity involves breaking out of established patterns in order to look at things in a different way.
>
> ~ *Edward de Bono*

We all get into habits and patterns; some of them are helping us and some are no longer serving us. As a leader, we must look at things differently and find creative solutions to each issue. What question can you ask yourself or your team to help you break an established pattern? Often a simple question such as "Does this pattern continue to serve our purposes? Is there a better way to do this? Why did we start doing it this way? How else can we do this?" is all it takes to spark your creativity and find a new solution.

Creativity/Innovation

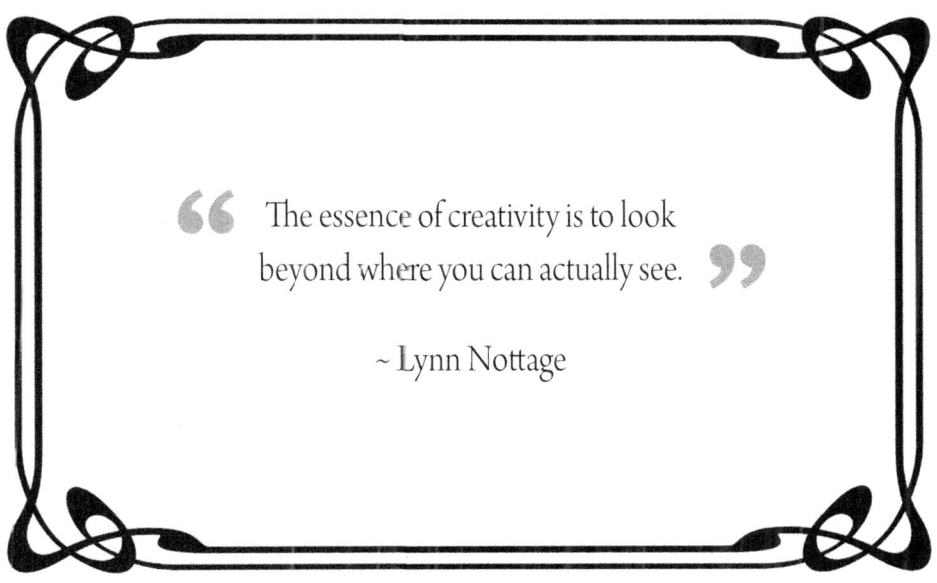

> "The essence of creativity is to look beyond where you can actually see."
>
> ~ Lynn Nottage

It is important as a leader to honestly assess a situation and see it clearly for what it is. Then use your creative ability to look beyond and see the possibilities. What possibilities and opportunities does your team have?

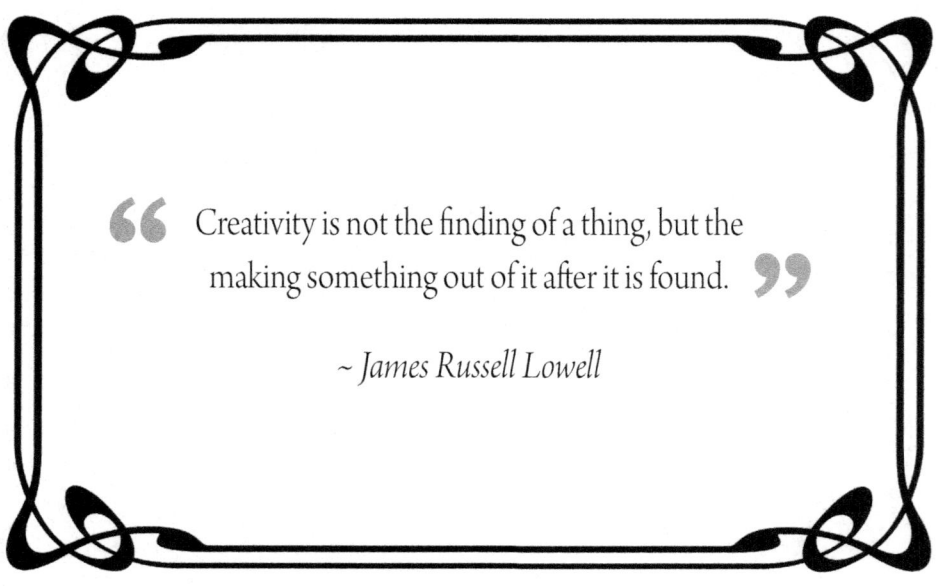

> Creativity is not the finding of a thing, but the making something out of it after it is found.
>
> ~ *James Russell Lowell*

Creative solutions require action. You may need a vision, or creative solution to resolve an issue, but without action, that vision or creative solution is wasted. This week, when you identify a creative solution to an issue - take action on that solution right away.

Creativity/Innovation

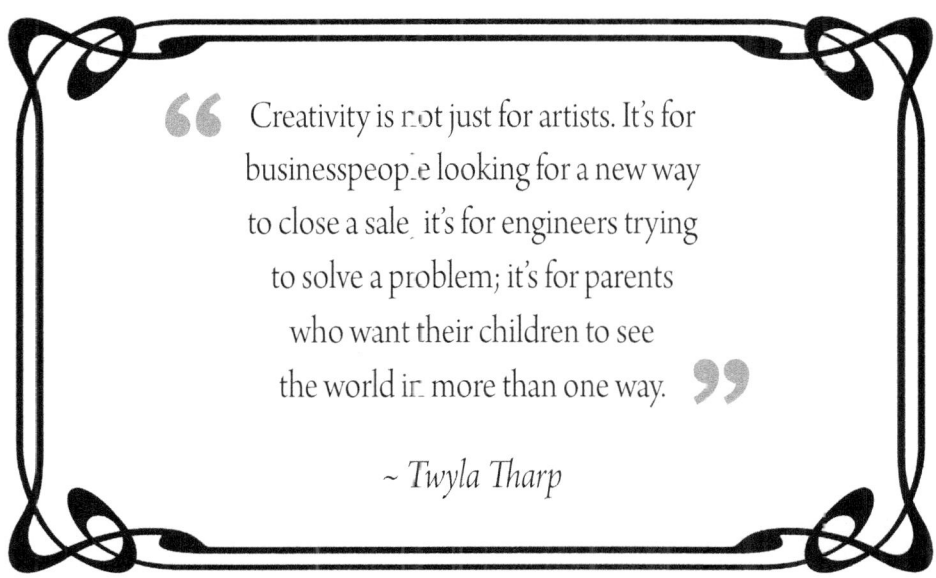

> " Creativity is not just for artists. It's for businesspeople looking for a new way to close a sale; it's for engineers trying to solve a problem; it's for parents who want their children to see the world in more than one way. "
>
> ~ *Twyla Tharp*

Leaders encourage their team to think creatively to resolve any issue. This week practice using your creativity to resolve issues in several different areas of your life. The more that you practice using creativity, the easier it is to think creatively when new situations come along.

Leadership In Action

> " For good ideas and true innovation, you need human interaction, conflict, argument, debate. "
>
> ~ *Margaret Heffernan*

Productive conflict and discussion sparks your brain to see things differently and consider new options. Where do you need innovation in your organization? Consider how you can create a safe environment for your team to have a discussion that includes healthy conflict to identify the best solutions.

Creativity/Innovation

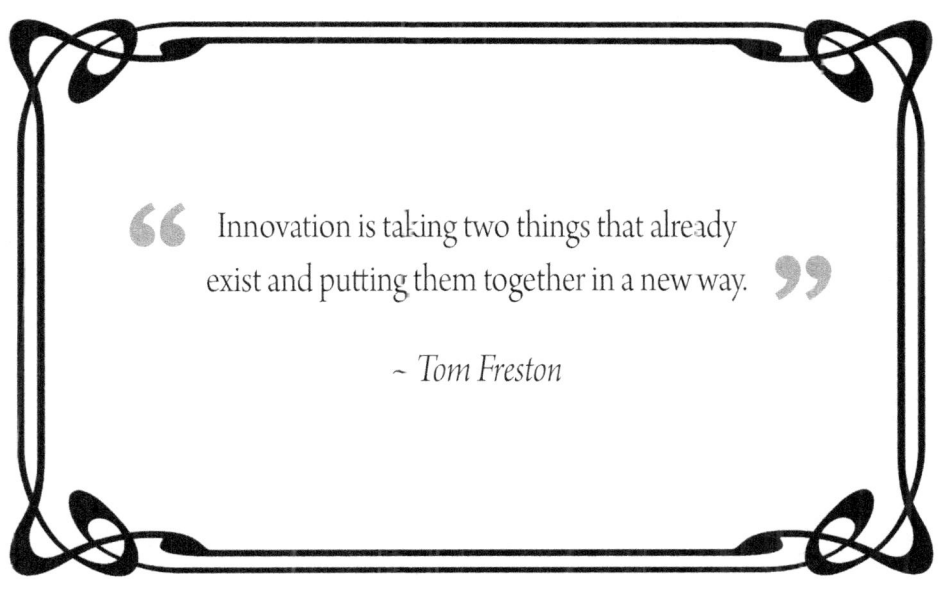

> " Innovation is taking two things that already exist and putting them together in a new way. "
>
> ~ Tom Freston

Leaders today need to be flexible thinkers, open to new solutions. Ask yourself this week, how can I take something I learned at a conference or in a meeting and apply it to new situations? What am I doing now that I can use in an unconventional way to create a new result?

Leadership In Action

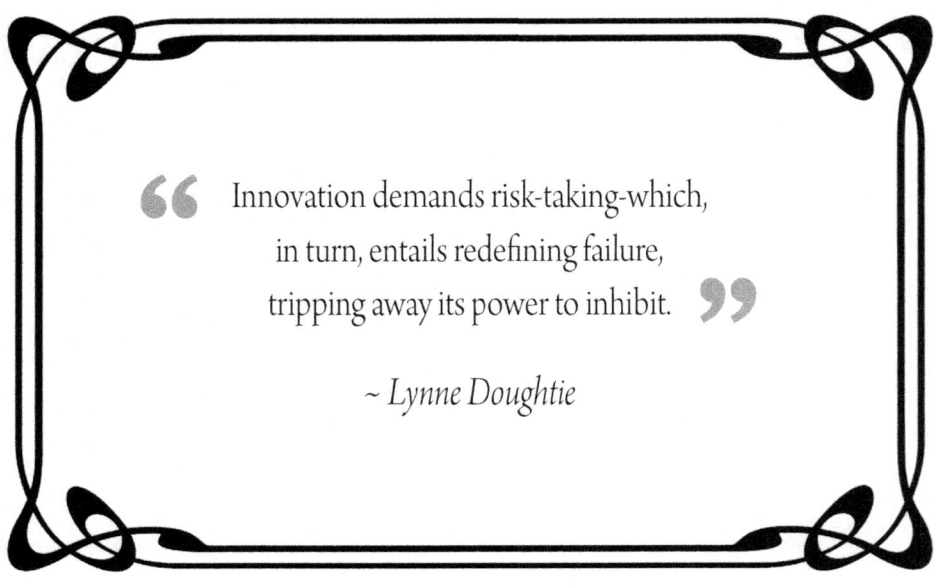

> " Innovation demands risk-taking-which, in turn, entails redefining failure, tripping away its power to inhibit. "
>
> ~ *Lynne Doughtie*

Trying something new always involves risk, so it is important to plan in advance for possible setbacks. How you interpret setbacks is the difference between moving forward with innovation and getting stuck. If things don't turn out as you thought, how can you redefine that setback? How can setbacks become an opportunity for improvements and learning?

Creativity/Innovation

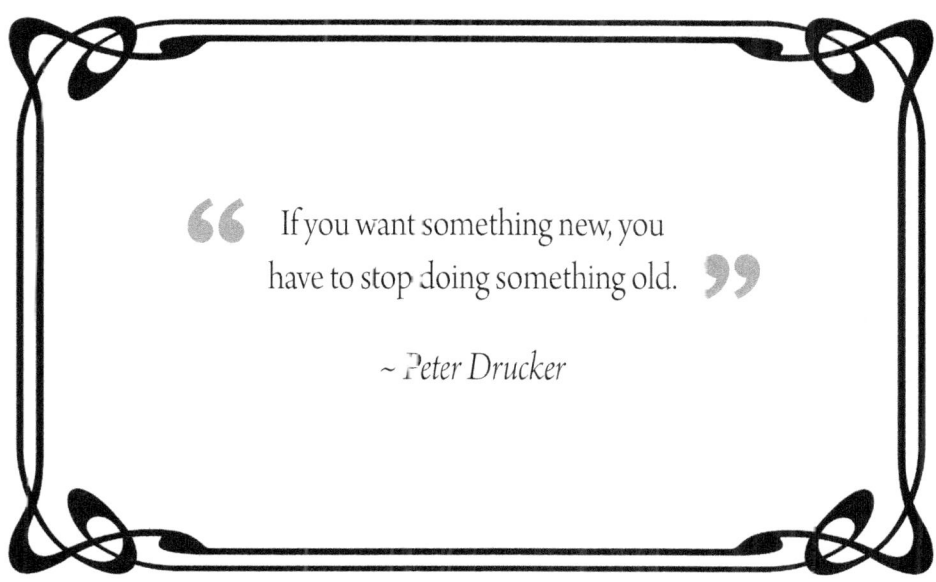

> " If you want something new, you have to stop doing something old. "
>
> ~ Peter Drucker

Innovation requires you to give up something to create something new. Think this week about what you would like to change and how willing you are to transform your current solution. Focus innovation on those things you are willing to change.

Leadership In Action

COLLABORATION/TEAMWORK

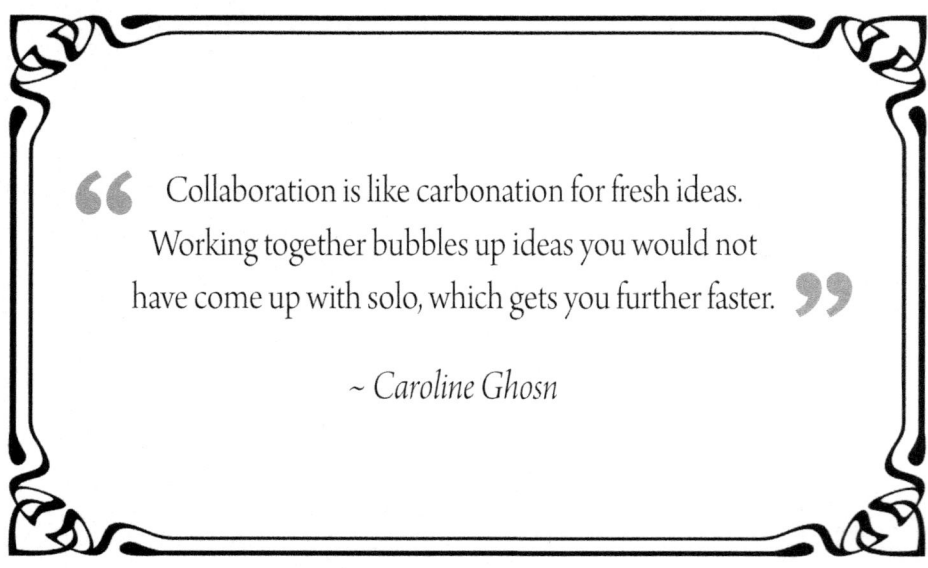

> " Collaboration is like carbonation for fresh ideas. Working together bubbles up ideas you would not have come up with solo, which gets you further faster. "
>
> ~ *Caroline Ghosn*

How you can add effervescence to your business ideas? Who can you collaborate with this week to make your ideas and their ideas sparkle? Schedule time to collaborate with others and make progress faster.

Collaboration/Teamwork

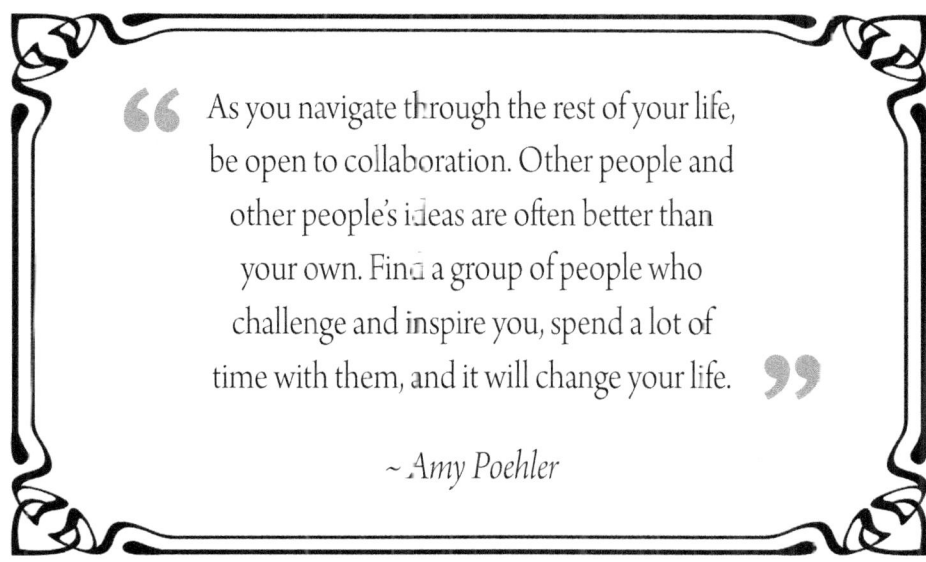

> As you navigate through the rest of your life, be open to collaboration. Other people and other people's ideas are often better than your own. Find a group of people who challenge and inspire you, spend a lot of time with them, and it will change your life.
>
> ~ Amy Poehler

Collaboration can be a catalyst for growth. Ask yourself who will challenge and inspire you and then plan to have a conversation with that person this week. How can you challenge and inspire them too?

Leadership In Action

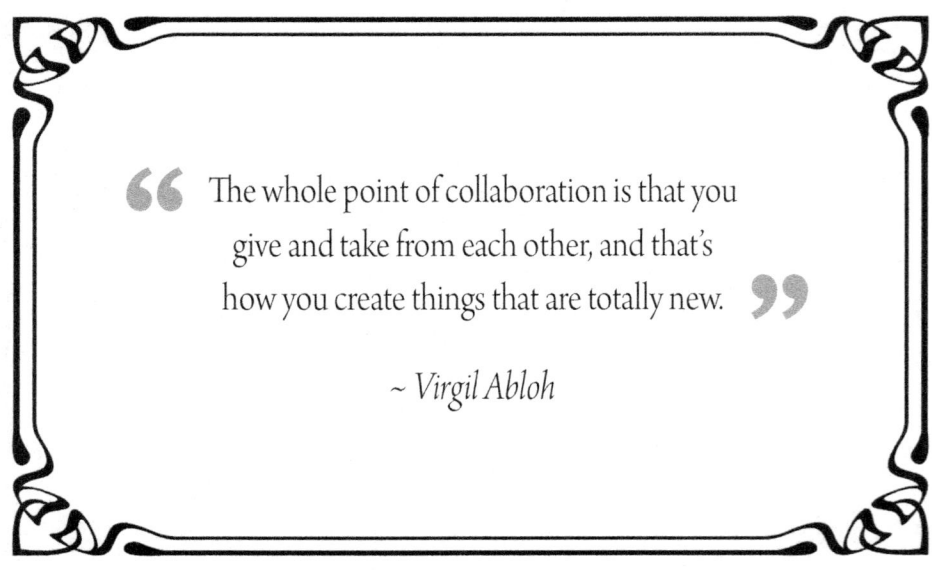

> **❝** The whole point of collaboration is that you give and take from each other, and that's how you create things that are totally new. **❞**
>
> *~ Virgil Abloh*

A conversation that inspires you to consider new ideas, and where you spark new ideas for others is like magic – suddenly you have possibilities that neither would have thought of alone. Ask a question in a meeting this week that will open new possibilities for everyone. Questions like "How else could we accomplish that result?" and "What could we accomplish if we did not have that limitation?" or "What is another way of thinking about this situation?" can spark new ideas.

Collaboration/Teamwork

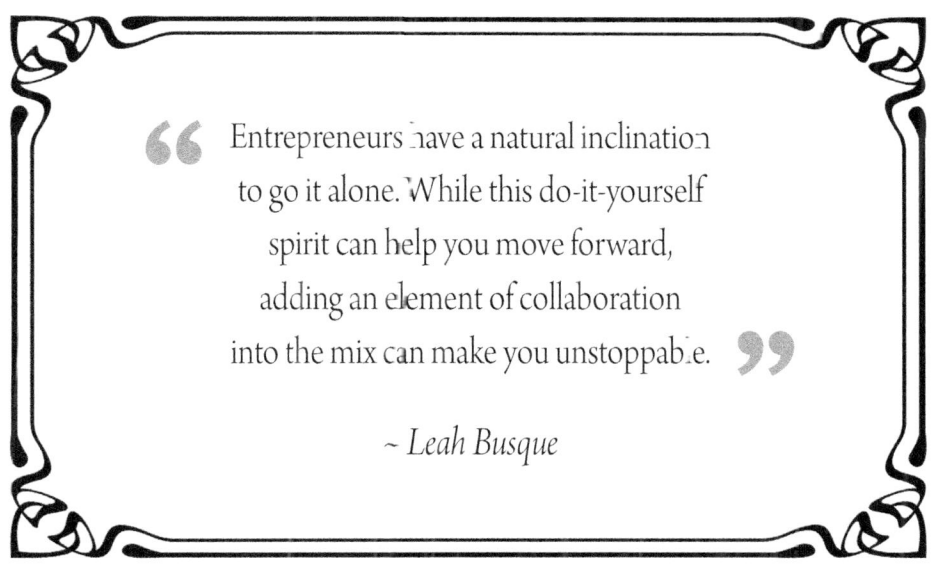

> "Entrepreneurs have a natural inclination to go it alone. While this do-it-yourself spirit can help you move forward, adding an element of collaboration into the mix can make you unstoppable."
>
> ~ Leah Busque

Whether you are an entrepreneur or an intrapreneur, this week, look at your annual plans and identify at least one action that you can collaborate on with someone else. Then reach out and begin a conversation.

> If you don't collaborate, your ideas will be limited to your own abilities.

Vishwas Chavan

 Differing perspectives and expanding ideas come from working with others. None of us can know everything and hearing other ideas will help spark new ideas in you. Who can you work with this week to brainstorm new solutions?

Collaboration/Teamwork

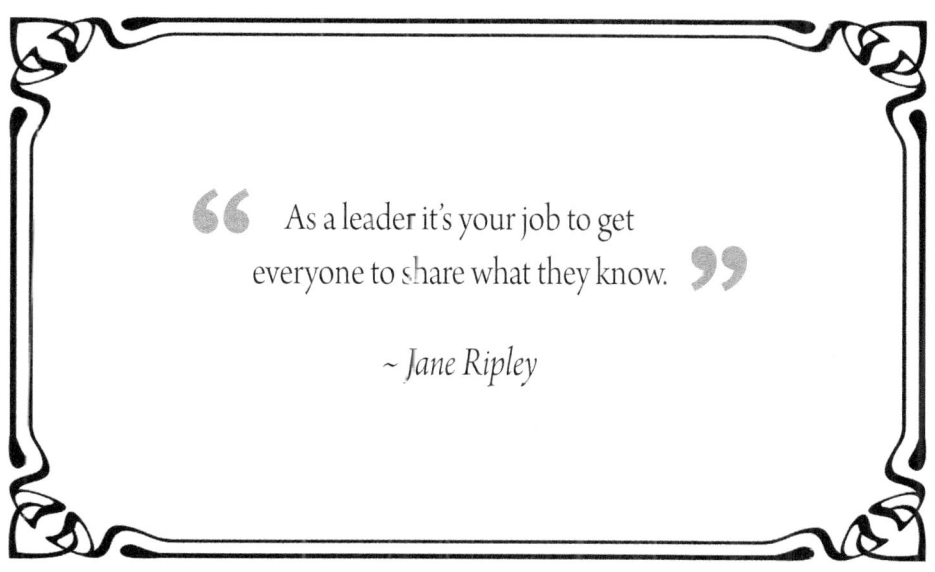

" As a leader it's your job to get everyone to share what they know. "

~ *Jane Ripley*

There are always some people on a team who remain quiet, but that doesn't mean they have nothing to contribute. Often the quiet members of a team are the deep thinkers. Consider this week how you can draw out those quiet team members and capture their ideas – you will be glad you did.

Leadership In Action

> " The nice thing about teamwork is you always have others on your side. "
>
> *~ Margaret Carty*

Teamwork is not just about sharing ideas. It is also about encouraging each other, boosting each other up when things are tough, and celebrating together when things go well. If you don't have a team yet, where can you find collaborators? If you have a strong team, what do you need to initiate next – boosting up, evaluating tough times, or celebrating?

Collaboration/Teamwork

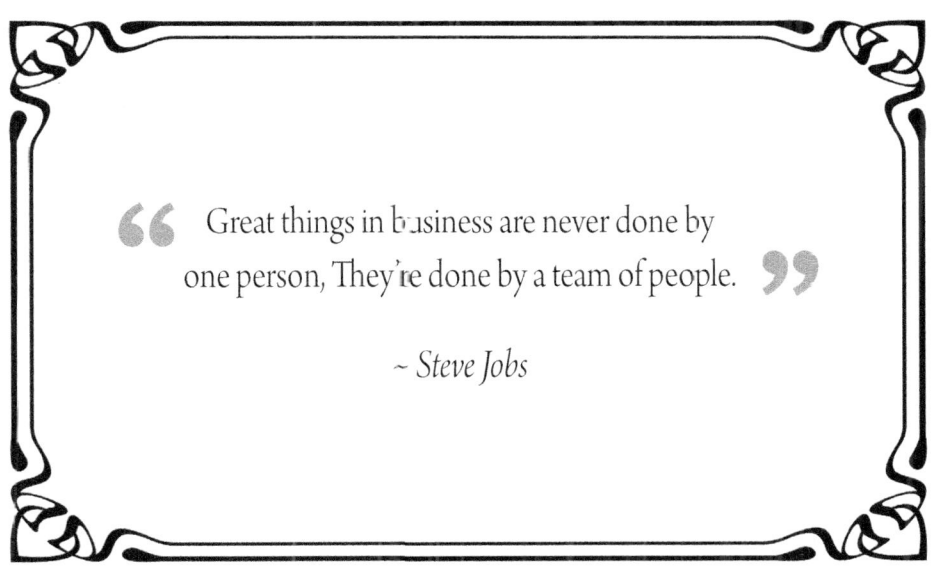

> Great things in business are never done by one person, They're done by a team of people.
>
> ~ Steve Jobs

There are many kinds of teams. Even if you are a solopreneur or an intrapreneur, you can develop a team of colleagues. Who do you need on your team so that you can do great things in your business?

Leadership In Action

POSITIVITY/POSSIBILITY

Leadership In Action

> " Successful people maintain a positive focus in life no matter what is going on around them. They stay focused on their past successes rather than their past failures, and on the next action steps they need to take to get them closer to the fulfillment of their goals rather than all the other distractions that life presents to them. "
>
> ~ *Jack Canfield*

As leaders, it is important to focus on the past successes of our teams and the next steps. With past failures, leaders focus on what they can learn from their mistakes and how best to use that learning. Consider this week, situations where you might not be focusing on successes or learning - how can you turn that around to keep you focused on action steps that move you closer to your goals?

Positivity/Possibility

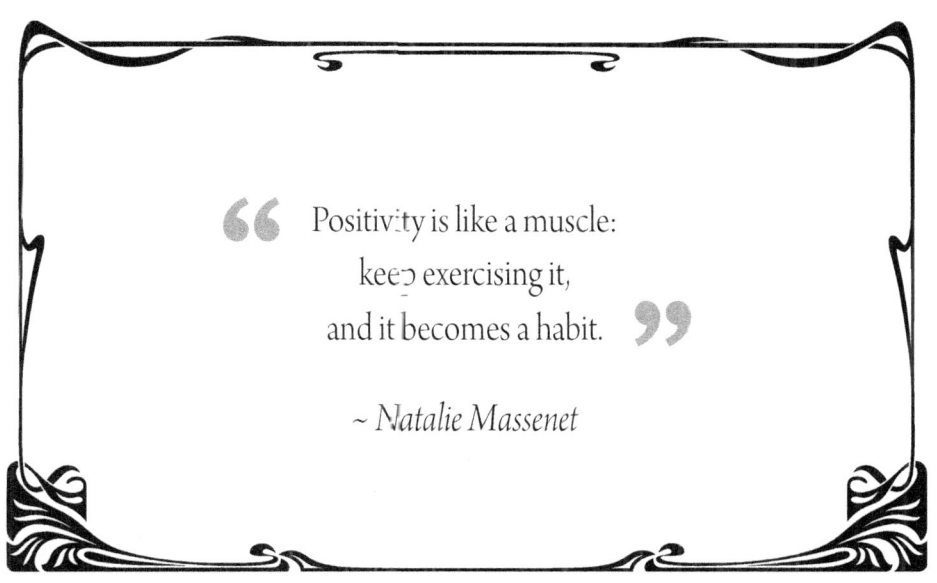

> "Positivity is like a muscle: keep exercising it, and it becomes a habit."
>
> ~ Natalie Massenet

How can we as leaders keep our focus on the positive? The more we look at the positive side of situations, the more positivity will become a habit. How could you create a daily practice of acknowledging the positive in your work or your life? Try it for a month and see if there is a change in your outlook.

Leadership In Action

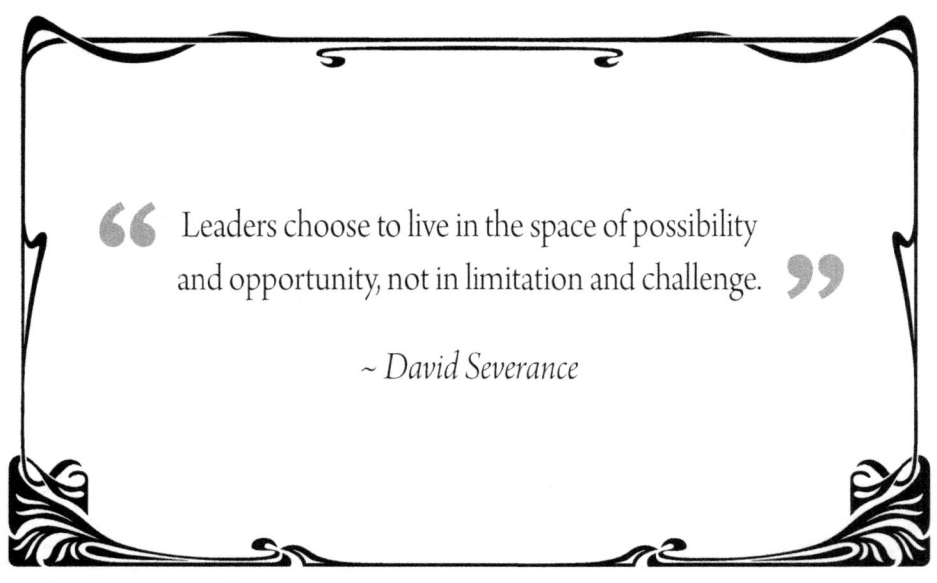

> "Leaders choose to live in the space of possibility and opportunity, not in limitation and challenge."
>
> ~ *David Severance*

It is difficult to move forward when you are thinking about limitations or challenges. Outstanding leaders see each situation with the thought "What is possible here? What are the opportunities?" Consider where you can ask yourself those questions this week to help you identify your next steps forward towards your goals.

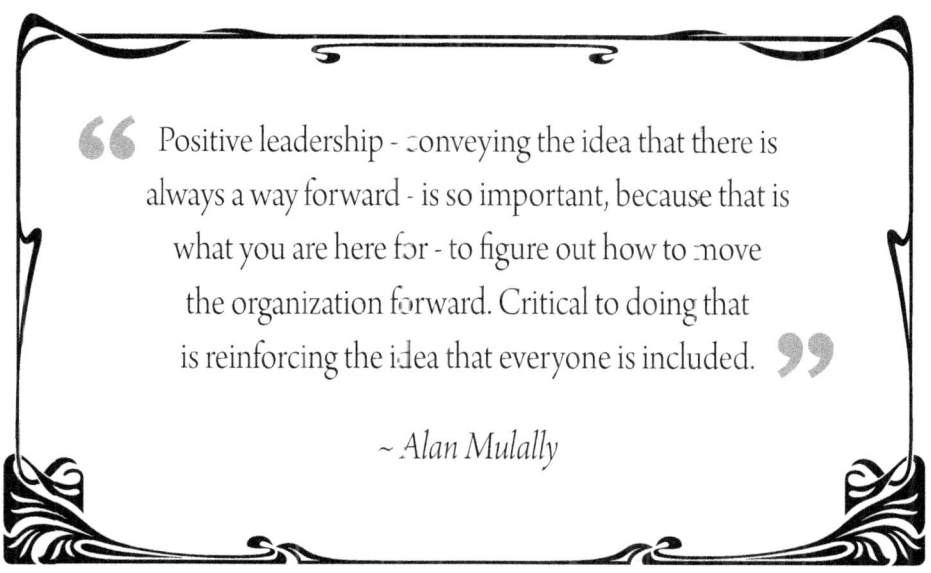

> Positive leadership - conveying the idea that there is always a way forward - is so important, because that is what you are here for - to figure out how to move the organization forward. Critical to doing that is reinforcing the idea that everyone is included.
>
> ~ Alan Mulally

As leaders, our job is to figure out how to move our organization forward from where we are right now, regardless of what has happened in the past. We are most successful when we enlist the help of our teams and inspire progress towards our goals.

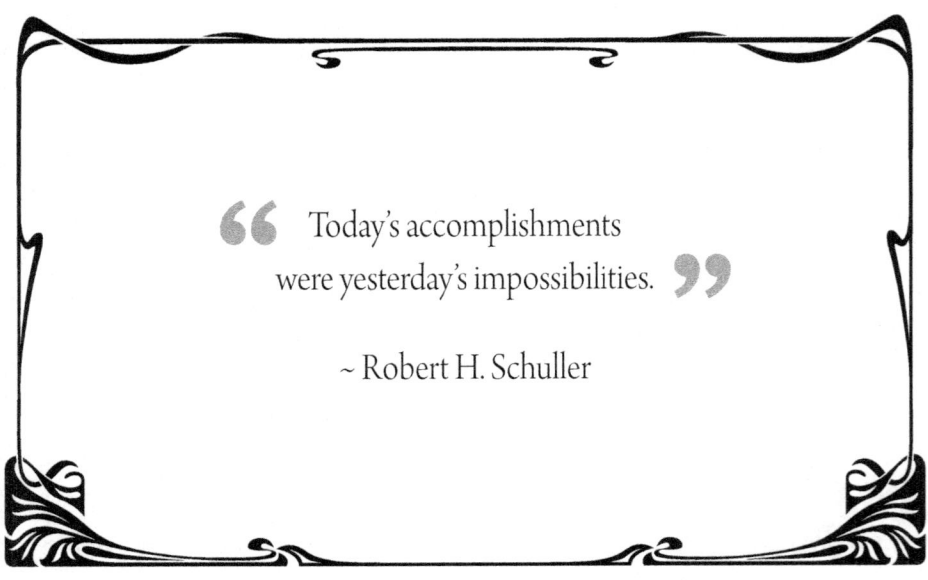

> Today's accomplishments were yesterday's impossibilities.
>
> ~ Robert H. Schuller

Often when we think of something as impossible, our brain stops creatively looking for a solution. But if you instead ask the question "How might that be possible?" your brain will start to work on solutions to that question. That will spark new ideas and you just may come up with a solution that is possible. Ask your team this week the question "How might that be possible?" and see what happens.

> "Take your mind off the problems for a moment, and focus on the positive possibilities. Consider how very much you are able to do."
>
> ~ Ralph Marston

As a leader, one way to influence your team is to take their minds off the current problems and get them to focus on the possibilities and what you can accomplish. Often that positive energy will spark ideas for how to resolve other problems and you will still be moving towards your goals.

Leadership In Action

> "What we find is that if you have a goal that is very, very far out, and you approach it in little steps, you start to get there faster. Your mind opens up to the possibilities."
>
> ~ *Mae Jemison*

 What is that very long-term goal you would like to reach? Can you start taking small steps towards that goal? Once you start to move in the direction of the goals you want to reach, your mind will spark with new ideas and possibilities and ways to get there faster.

Positivity, Possibility

> " If we can see past preconceived limitations, then the possibilities are endless. "
>
> ~ Amy Purdy

It is easy to get stuck on our preconceived limitations. As a leader, it's important to help our team think beyond those limitations and consider the possibilities. Ask your team "What is limiting our thinking on this matter?" "What are the possibilities?"

Leadership In Action

INTENTION/COMMITMENT

Leadership In Action

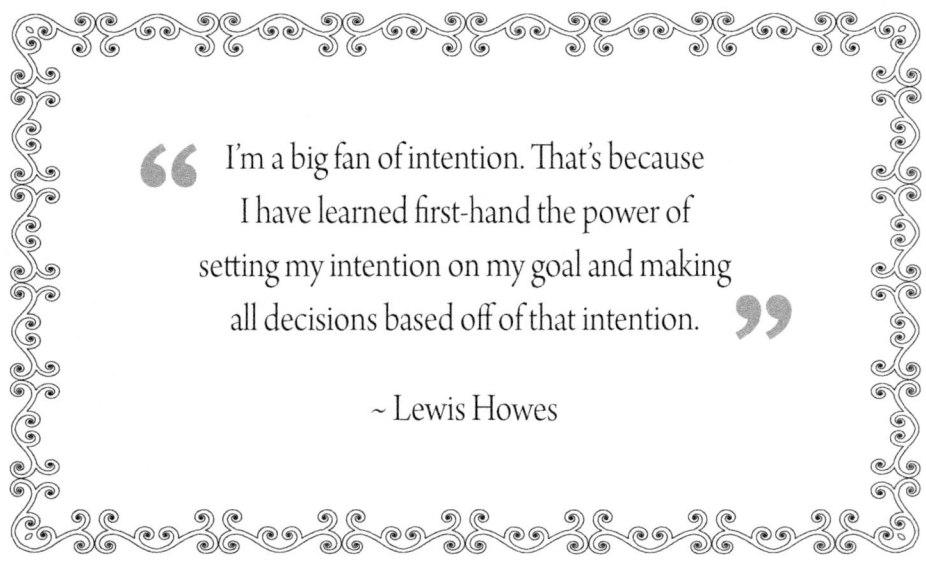

> " I'm a big fan of intention. That's because I have learned first-hand the power of setting my intention on my goal and making all decisions based off of that intention. "
>
> ~ Lewis Howes

Setting intentions for each meeting or project is one way that leaders stay focused on the outcome they are trying to achieve. They think carefully about the best outcome and know that their ideas are not the only ones to be considered. Do you have a difficult meeting coming up? Try setting an intention for a win-win solution and see how that affects your interaction in the meeting.

Intention/Commitment

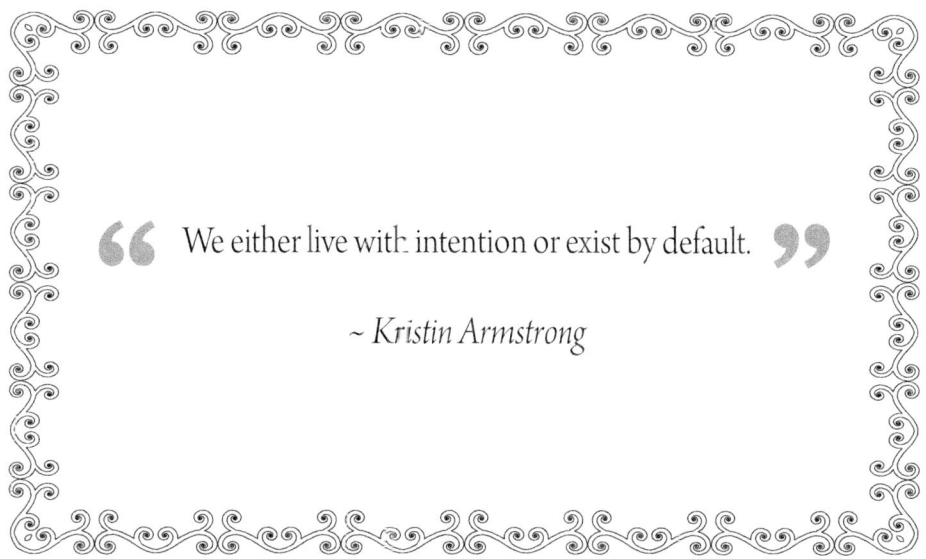

> We either live with intention or exist by default.
>
> ~ Kristin Armstrong

When leaders go into a meeting or project without intention, they are in default mode and reacting to what happens rather than looking for ways to create the best outcome. Successful leaders regularly set intentions for the outcome of their work. To practice setting intentions this week, try setting an intention for a conversation such as "I am meeting with John today – I am curious about how I can help him with his new project." How might that change the conversation?

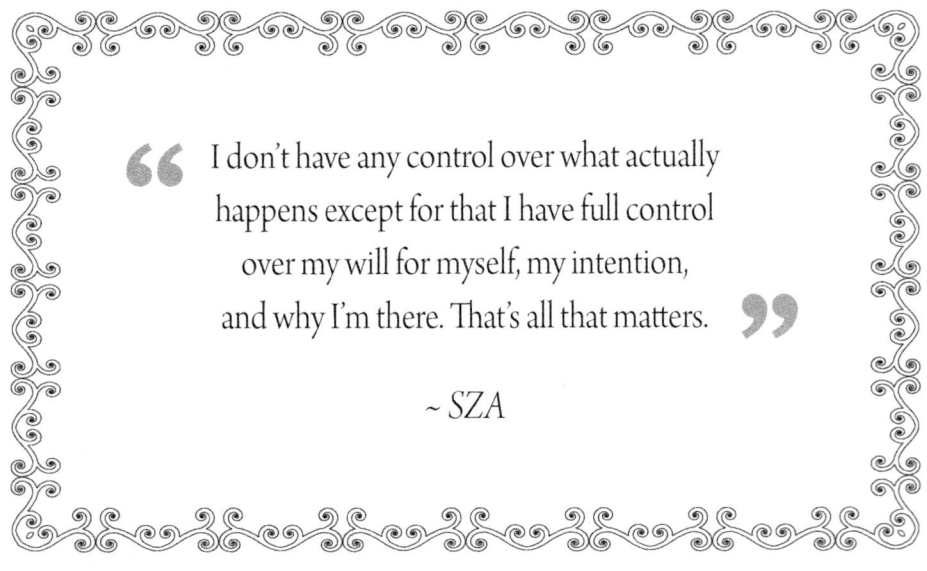

> " I don't have any control over what actually happens except for that I have full control over my will for myself, my intention, and why I'm there. That's all that matters. "
>
> ~ SZA

While we don't have control over the outcome, setting an intention and staying focused on that intention gives you leverage to influence the outcome. How can you stay focused with intention this week?

Intention/Commitment

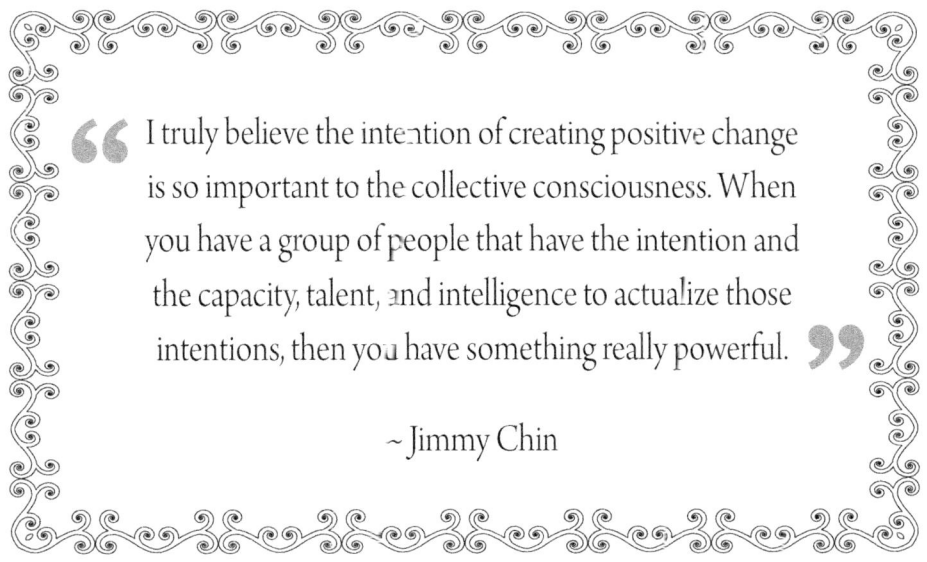

> I truly believe the intention of creating positive change is so important to the collective consciousness. When you have a group of people that have the intention and the capacity, talent, and intelligence to actualize those intentions, then you have something really powerful.
>
> ~ Jimmy Chin

Setting an intention together with your team can help create very powerful outcomes. Suddenly, you have the whole team focused on the best solution for the meeting or project. Try it out this week and see what happens.

Leadership In Action

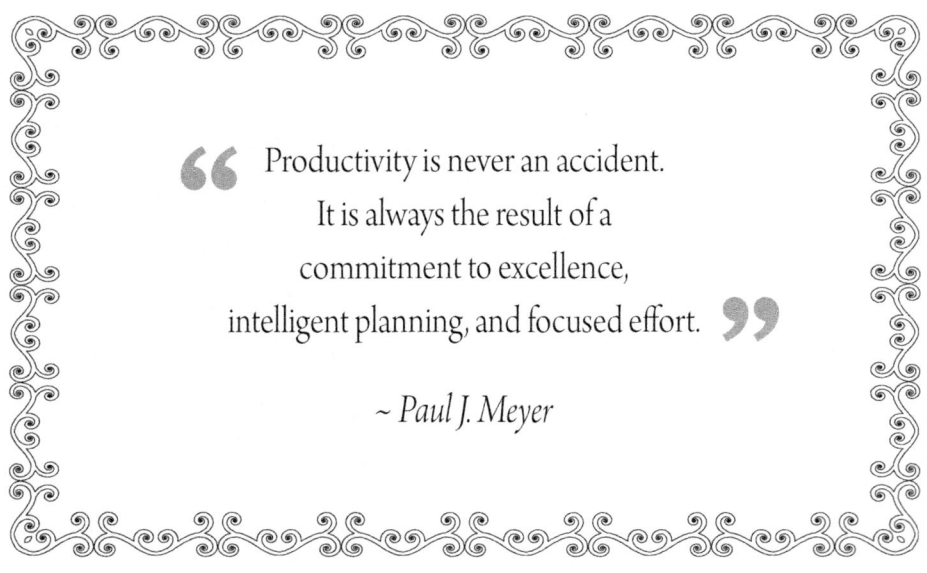

> " Productivity is never an accident.
> It is always the result of a
> commitment to excellence,
> intelligent planning, and focused effort. "
>
> ~ *Paul J. Meyer*

In this uncharted time, with everyone learning new ways to work and communicate, it is even more important to commit to our desired outcomes. It is the commitment to the outcome that will ensure productivity. Take some time this week to clarify the outcome you are looking for and commit to creating that outcome. It may not happen the way you originally planned, but you can still reach that goal.

Intention/Commitment

> " Commitment is what transforms a promise into a reality. "
>
> ~ *Abraham Lincoln*

Where have you made a promise recently - have you asked yourself how committed you are to making that promise a reality. Often in business, we make promises that we will most likely not be able to keep - a deadline to get a specific task done when we know our plate is full; a promise to follow up with a call tomorrow when we know we have an extremely busy day the next day; a promise to devote a half-hour with a colleague reviewing a product or service when you know you don't have time on your calendar to meet that day, etc. When you make a promise, ask yourself how committed you are to turning that promise into reality. If you are committed, it is much more likely to happen. If not, maybe you should revise your promise. Making a commitment and successfully achieving the reality of the promise helps to build trust.

Leadership In Action

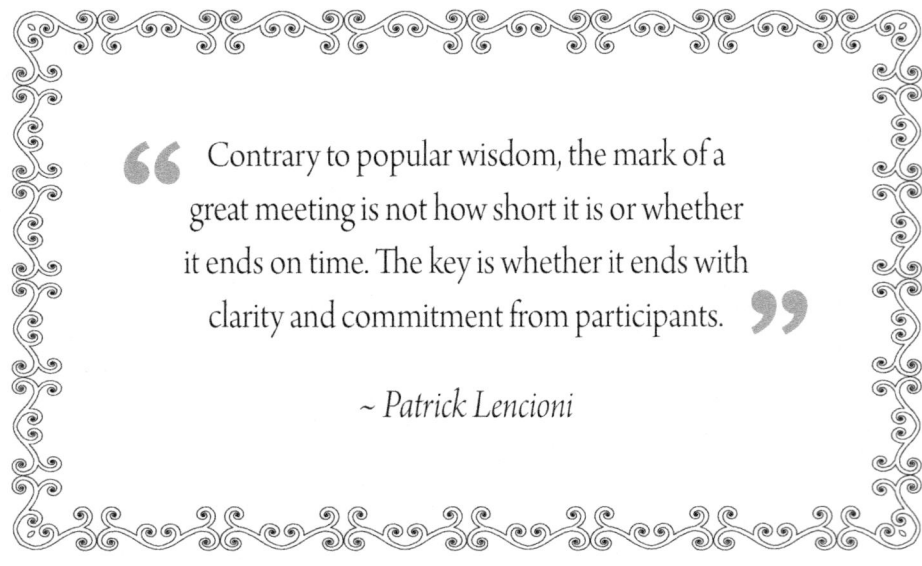

> " Contrary to popular wisdom, the mark of a great meeting is not how short it is or whether it ends on time. The key is whether it ends with clarity and commitment from participants. "
>
> ~ *Patrick Lencioni*

In these times of virtual meetings, many people are being more efficient with their time, and meetings are shorter, but have they ended with clarity? Ask yourself this week, "Is everyone clear about the next steps from this meeting? Do we all have the same vision for the next steps? Is everyone committed to their part in these next steps?" Working towards clarity and commitment to the next steps is what will make the meeting a great meeting.

Intention/Commitment

> " Motivation is what gets you started.
> Commitment is what keeps you going. "
>
> ~ Jim Rohn

How many of us have gotten excited about an idea and started along the path to making it a reality, but we hit a snag or stumbling block. Your commitment to the outcome will keep you focused on the actions you need to take when things get difficult. When starting something new, ask yourself "where might I/we get stuck trying to achieve this challenge? What do we need to commit to in order to keep our team motivated?

Leadership In Action

PREPARATION/PLANNING

Leadership In Action

> " I feel that luck is preparation meeting opportunity. "
>
> ~ *Oprah Winfrey*

With the new year upon us, we all look forward to a happy and successful year and wish for some luck as well. When those opportunities cross your path this year, will you be ready? What can you set in motion today to be certain that you and your team are prepared when that opportunity comes along?

Preparation/Planning

> "One important key to success is self-confidence. An important key to self-confidence is preparation."
>
> ~ Arthur Ash

 What could you or your team accomplish if you were confident in your ability to succeed? Self-confidence is important to every team, in every endeavor. In what areas is your team lacking self-confidence? Where could preparation help build your team's confidence? What can you do to help your team be better prepared and, therefore, confident when addressing the challenges, events, or projects ahead?

Leadership In Action

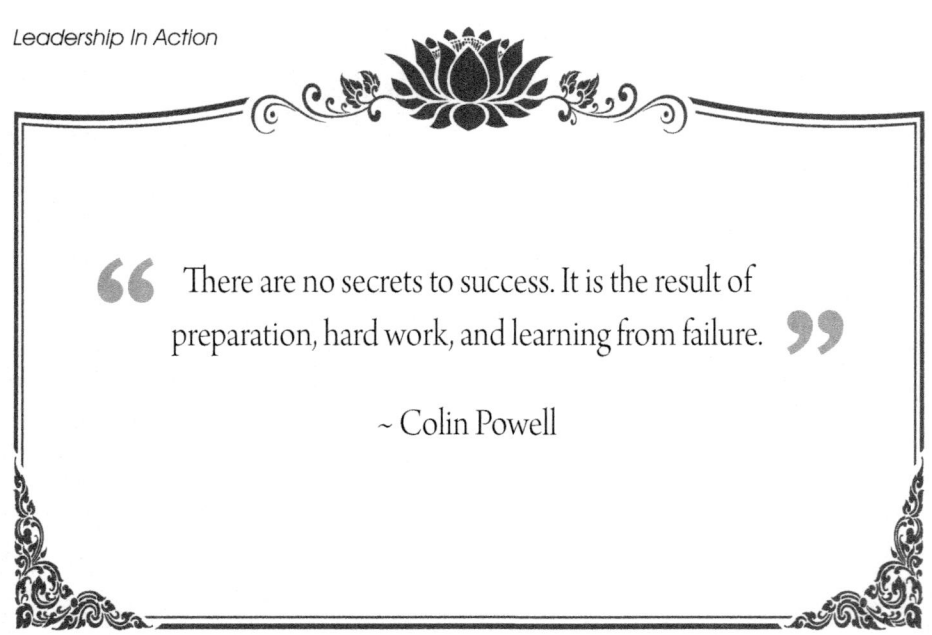

> " There are no secrets to success. It is the result of preparation, hard work, and learning from failure. "
>
> ~ Colin Powell

Are you taking the time to prepare for your success? This week, ask your team where they would like to be better prepared, then prioritize and make time for preparation.

Preparation/Planning

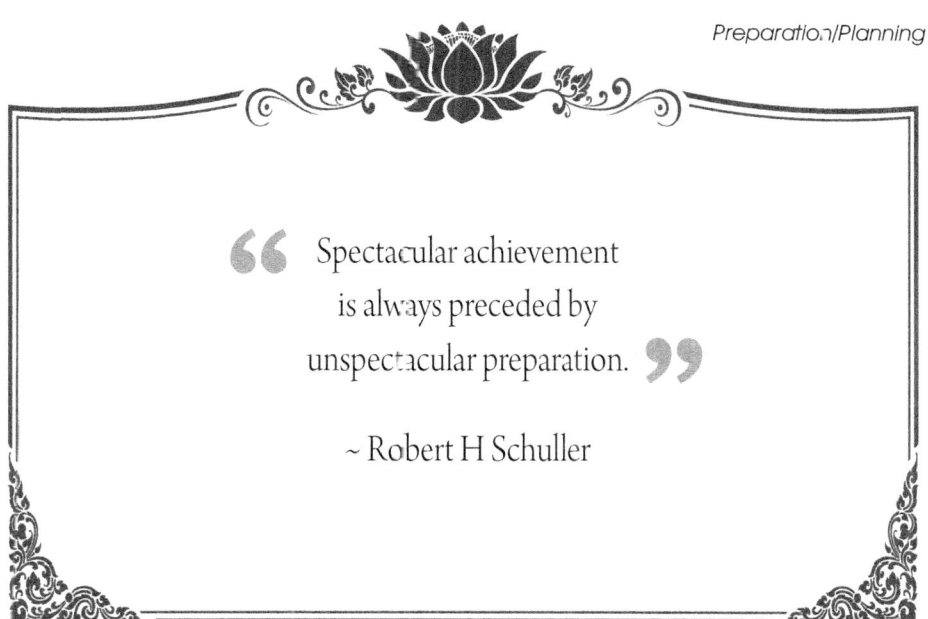

> " Spectacular achievement
> is always preceded by
> unspectacular preparation. "
>
> ~ Robert H Schuller

Where might you be getting by without preparation? What could you achieve if you spent time in preparation? Choose one place to be spectacular this week, and dedicate an hour or two in preparation that will bring you even greater success.

Leadership In Action

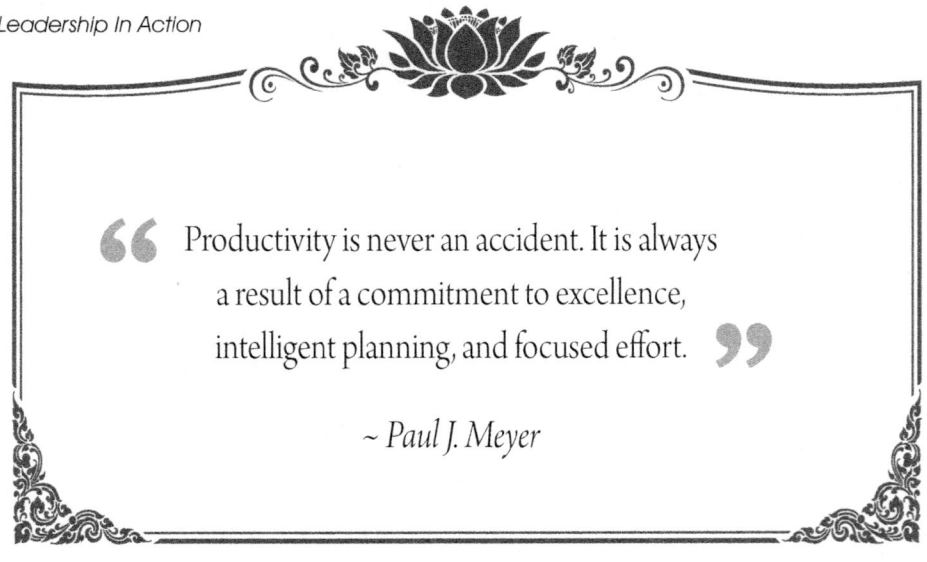

> " Productivity is never an accident. It is always a result of a commitment to excellence, intelligent planning, and focused effort. "
>
> *~ Paul J. Meyer*

Leaders are often asked to increase productivity with their team, but it is not as simple as asking the team to work harder. As leaders, we need to plan and communicate how we define excellence in the work our team performs while also being productive. Planning, followed by a focused effort from your team, will result in increased productivity. How completely have you defined the desired excellent outcome you are looking for? How will you use that definition to keep your team productive and focused on the right things?

Preparation/Planning

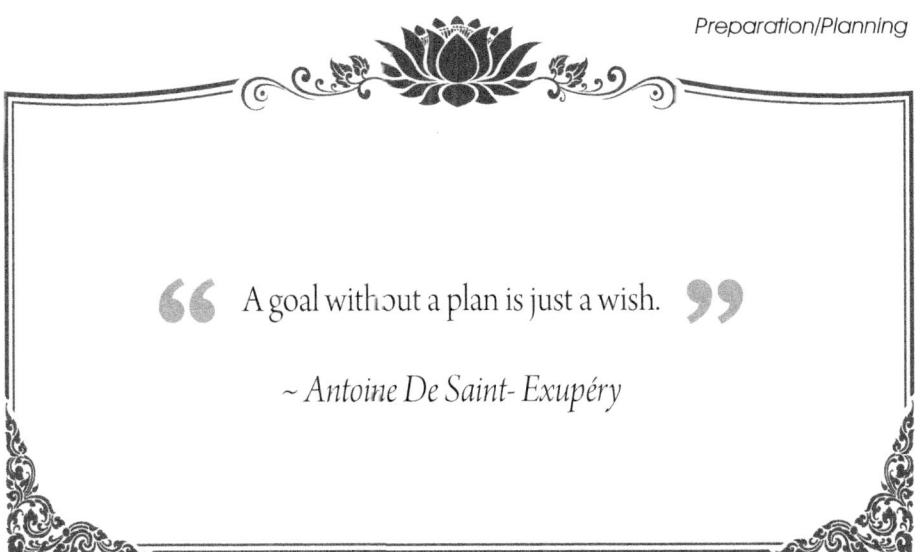

" A goal without a plan is just a wish. "

~ Antoine De Saint- Exupéry

As a leader, it is important to set goals, but if you don't also identify and follow the steps to achieve that goal, you are much less likely to be successful. What goals do you have for the year? Spend time this week to identify the steps you need to accomplish to achieve those goals.

Leadership In Action

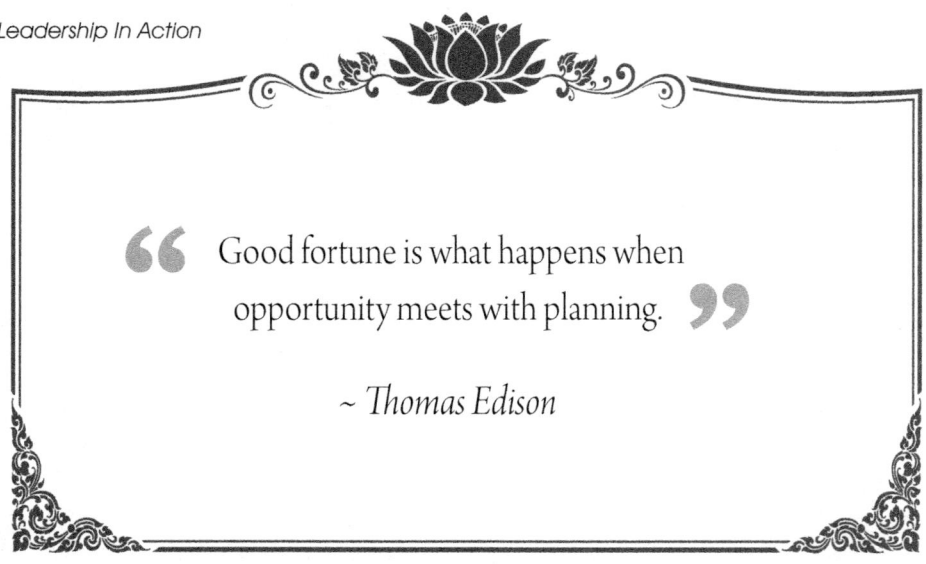

> Good fortune is what happens when opportunity meets with planning.
>
> ~ *Thomas Edison*

Leaders, like sports coaches, need to prepare their team for the opportunities that may come in the future. In team sports, you never know what plays the opposing team will make, so the team must prepare for as many plays as possible. When the opponent makes that play, the team is ready with a plan to respond. It is the same in business, you never know what opportunities will come your way, being as prepared as possible will put you in a position to take advantage of those opportunities when they come up. What is one thing you can do between now and the end of the year to prepare for future opportunities?

CONSISTENCY

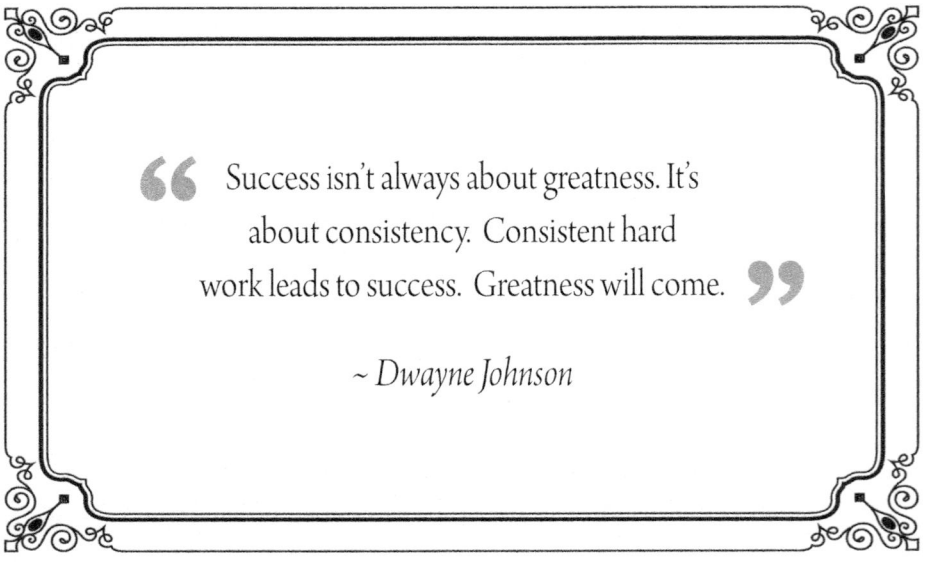

As leaders, we strive for success, but it is consistently working towards success and doing the right things that allow us to achieve success. This week consider where you and your team are most consistent, and where are you least consistent. Are you being consistent with the right things?

Consistency

> " For me, the challenge isn't to be different but to be consistent. "
>
> ~ Joan Jett

It is relatively easy to do something once, and move on, but much more challenging to be consistent, to do something over and over again, and maintain a consistent quality each time. This is the challenge of a leader, find the right things to do consistently, and then maintain a consistent quality every time you do it.

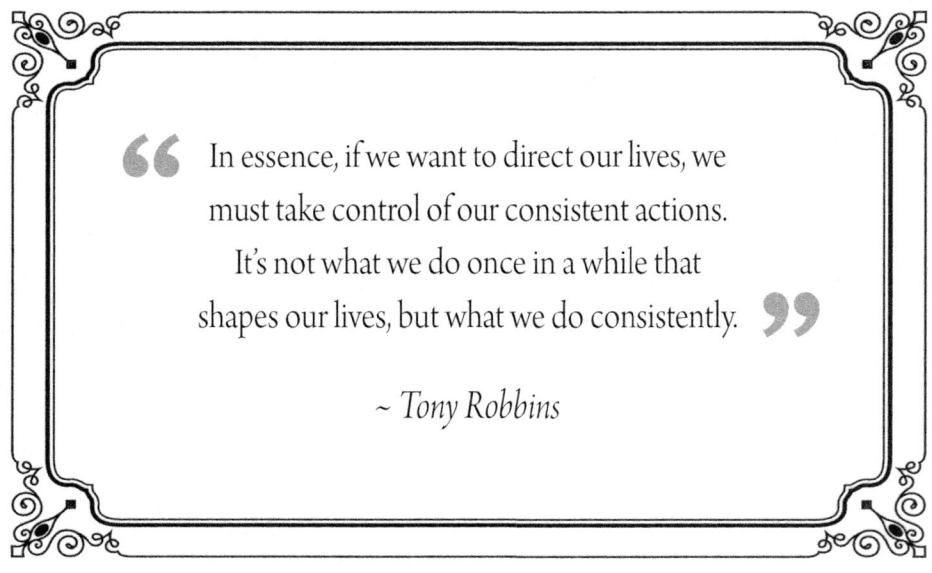

> In essence, if we want to direct our lives, we must take control of our consistent actions. It's not what we do once in a while that shapes our lives, but what we do consistently.
>
> ~ Tony Robbins

To "take control of our consistent actions" - What are your consistent actions? Are they leading you and your team towards the successful outcome that you are striving for? What is one small change you can do consistently that will elevate the work of the whole team?

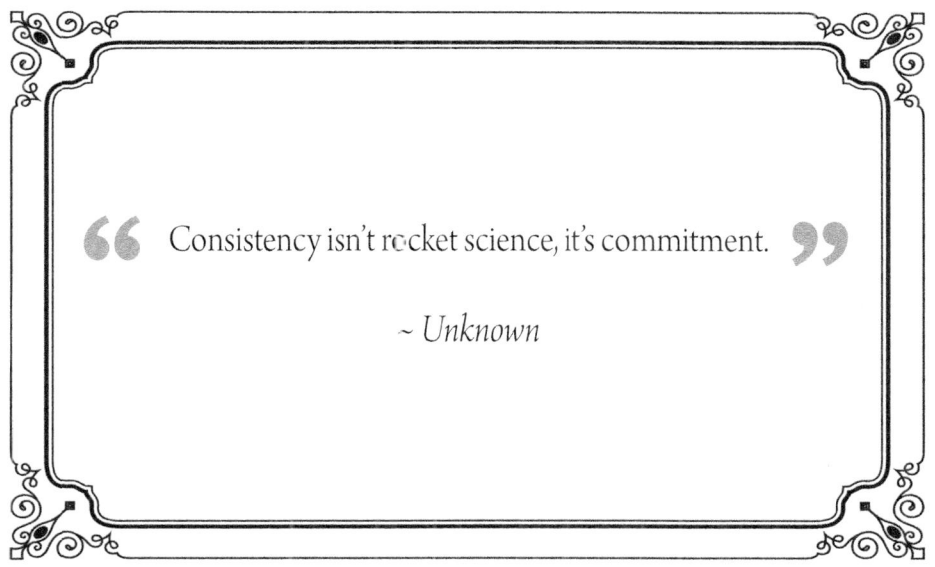

> "Consistency isn't rocket science, it's commitment."
>
> ~ *Unknown*

When you are planning for consistent actions to move you forward, it doesn't need to be complicated, but it does take commitment. This is about planning for a marathon of actions. What will inspire you and your team to take consistent action towards your goal? How can you prepare your team for the marathon of action that is required? How can you make it simple enough that you and your team comply?

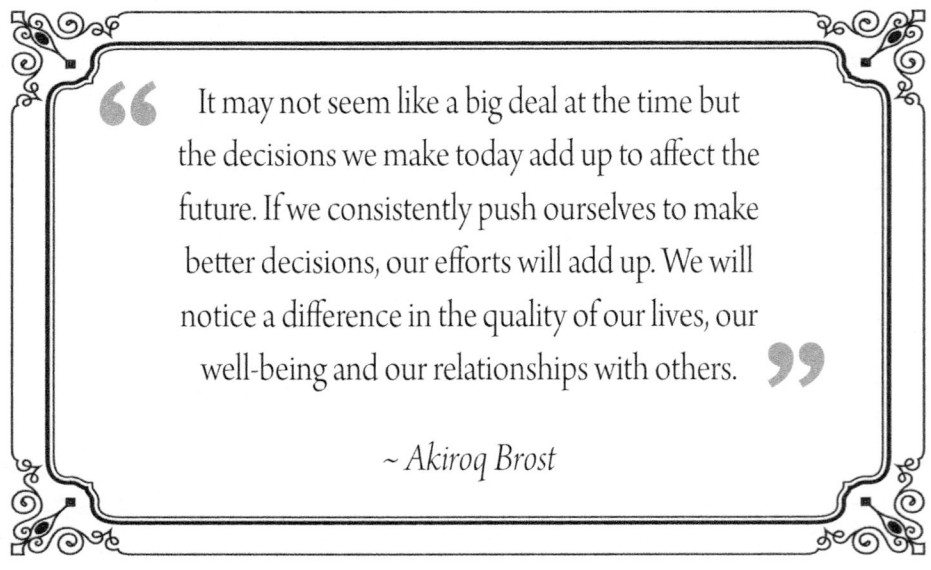

> "It may not seem like a big deal at the time but the decisions we make today add up to affect the future. If we consistently push ourselves to make better decisions, our efforts will add up. We will notice a difference in the quality of our lives, our well-being and our relationships with others."
>
> ~ Akiroq Brost

What if you consistently encouraged your team to make better decisions? Would you see a difference in your business? As a leader, our responsibility is to ask questions to lead the team to better decisions. What question can you ask this week that will lead you to a better decision?

> Success is the sum of small efforts,
> repeated day-in and day-out.
>
> ~ *Robert Collier*

 Consider the small efforts you do every day, and repeat them day after day. What are they leading you to? Will they keep you or your organization on the right path to success? What small new consistent effort could you create that will bring you towards your success?

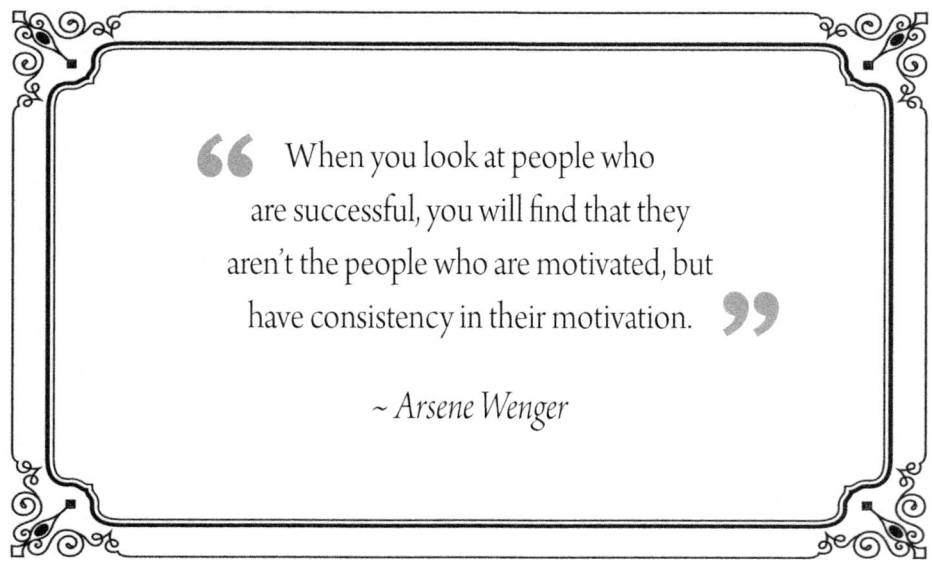

> " When you look at people who are successful, you will find that they aren't the people who are motivated, but have consistency in their motivation. "
>
> ~ Arsene Wenger

Motivation is important, but the continuous effort in the right direction is most likely to help you achieve your goals. Consider what you can begin this week and continue with for a very long time that takes you towards your ultimate outcome. Don't do it alone, how can you enlist your team to help you?

Consistency

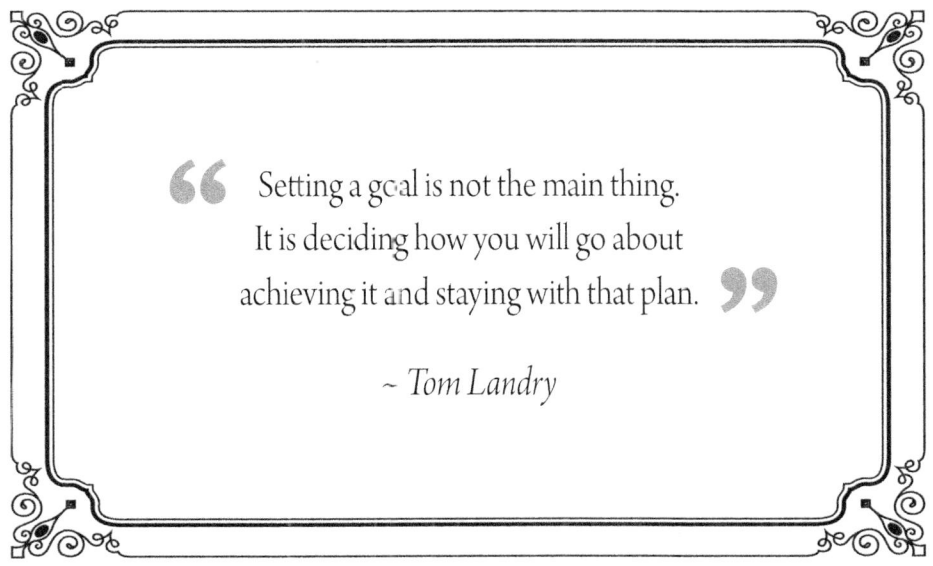

> " Setting a goal is not the main thing.
> It is deciding how you will go about
> achieving it and staying with that plan. "
>
> ~ Tom Landry

Setting goals is important, but having an action plan to achieve those goals is even more important. What are the actions you and your team are taking that lead you to your goals? What small actions could you add that will help you and your team get there?

Leadership In Action

PASSION/PURPOSE

> "Passion is energy. Feel the power that comes from focusing on what excited you."
>
> ~ *Oprah Winfrey*

When leaders focus on their passion, it raises their energy in all areas of their business and their life. Take some time to reconnect with your passion for your work. Observe what difference it makes for you and your interactions with those around you.

Passion/Purpose

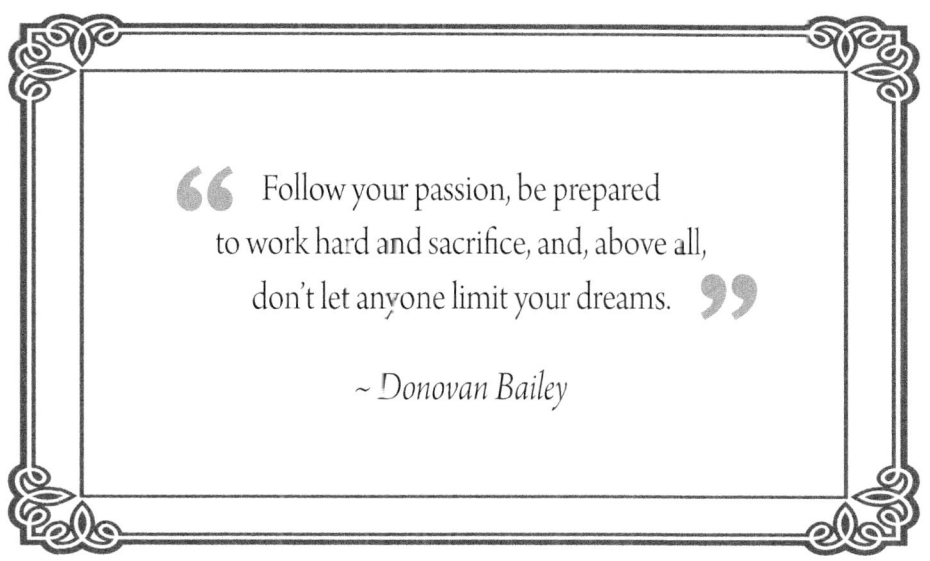

> Follow your passion, be prepared to work hard and sacrifice, and, above all, don't let anyone limit your dreams.
>
> ~ Donovan Bailey

Leaders can have the greatest impact when they are acting through their passion. Passion and hard work combined can help you to reach your dreams. Tap into that passion this week to motivate you through the hard work and bring yourself closer to your dreams.

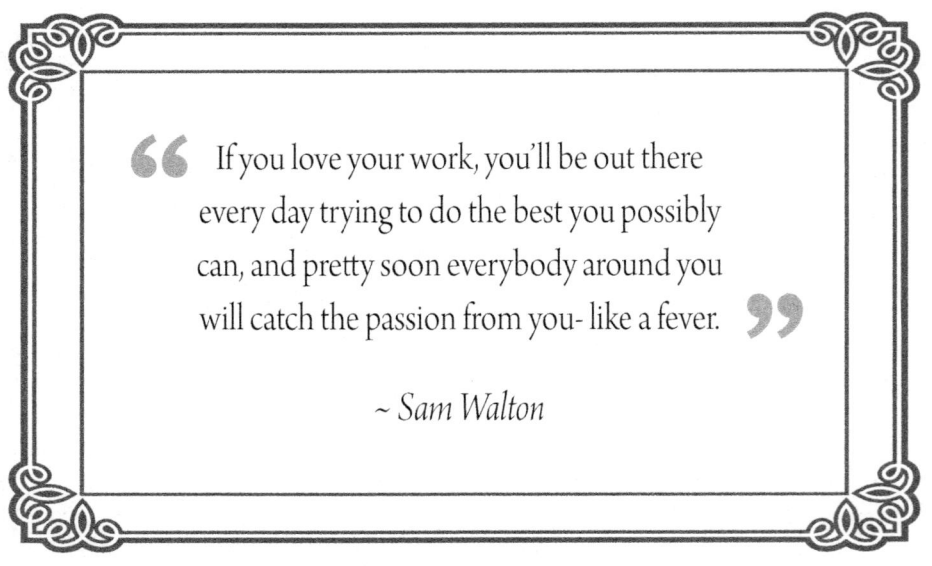

> " If you love your work, you'll be out there every day trying to do the best you possibly can, and pretty soon everybody around you will catch the passion from you- like a fever. "
>
> ~ Sam Walton

Working with someone who is passionate about what they are doing is infectious. When leaders focus on communicating their passion for the work they are doing, they can raise the energy in all those around them. How are you communicating your passion in all areas of your life?

Passion/Purpose

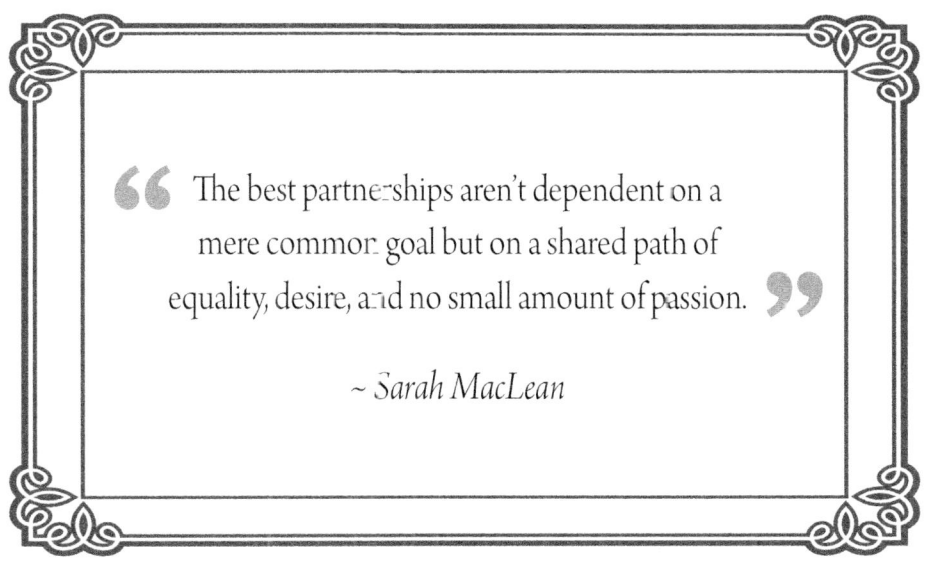

> " The best partnerships aren't dependent on a mere common goal but on a shared path of equality, desire, and no small amount of passion. "
>
> ~ Sarah MacLean

Inspired partnerships rely on passion for a shared goal to elevate the outcome of the partnership. Bringing passion into their business partnerships helps great leaders have an impact on others around them. Where is your passion for a specific goal or outcome working in your business relationships?

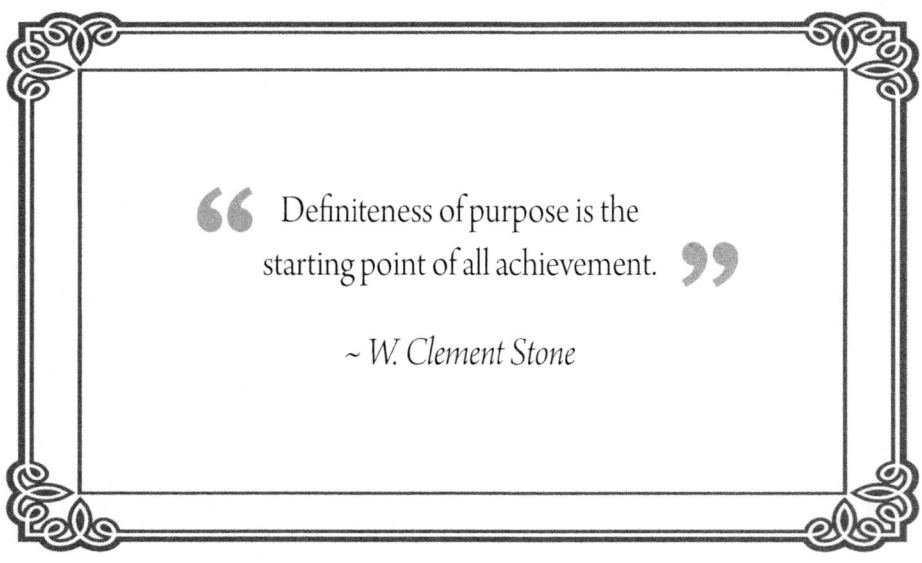

> "Definiteness of purpose is the starting point of all achievement."
>
> ~ W. Clement Stone

Leaders who are very clear about the purpose of what they are doing, inspire and influence those around them. Take a few minutes today to focus on your purpose and how to share it with others.

Passion/Purpose

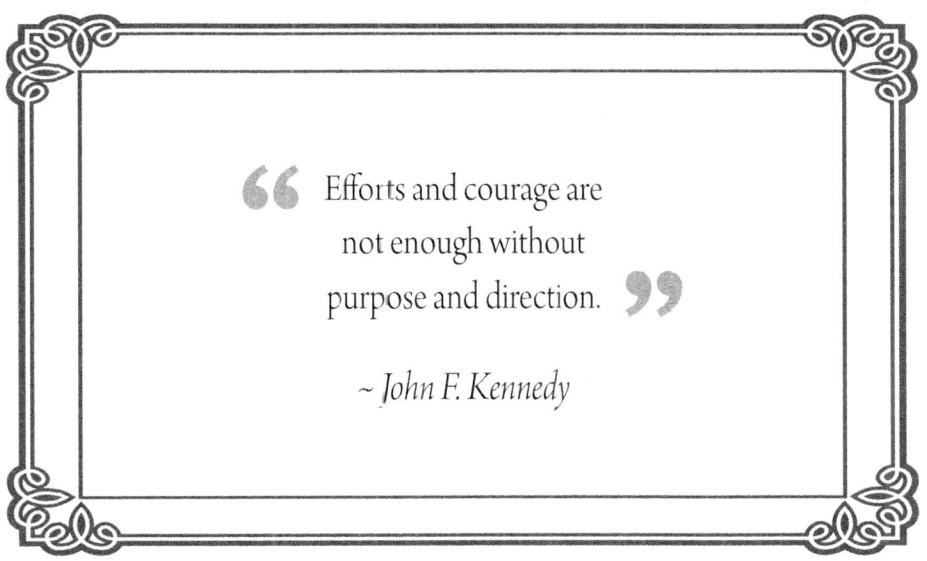

> Efforts and courage are not enough without purpose and direction.
>
> ~ *John F. Kennedy*

Most of us have had the experience of working hard on something that didn't reach its full potential or turned out not to be the solution. Taking the time to define the purpose and direction of what you are doing first will augment your efforts and be more satisfying. Which project this week would benefit from you taking the time to clarify the purpose?

Leadership In Action

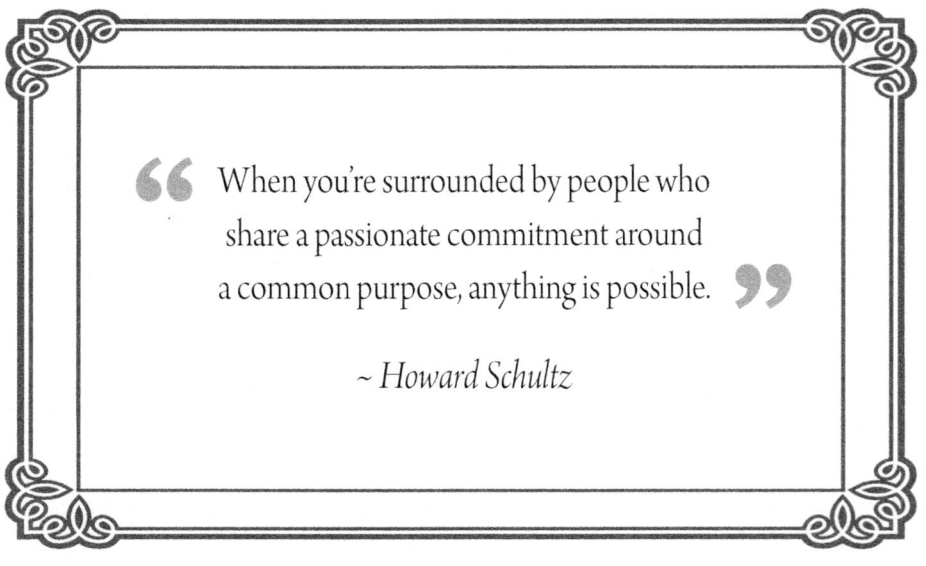

> 66 When you're surrounded by people who share a passionate commitment around a common purpose, anything is possible. 99
>
> ~ *Howard Schultz*

As leaders, it is our job to communicate our passion and purpose to those around us. When we have everyone committed and passionate about a common purpose, it is amazing what we can accomplish. Have a conversation this week with a client or colleague and share your passion, commitment and purpose.

> " As a leader, you must consistently drive effective communication. Meetings must be deliberate and intentional - your organizational rhythm should value purpose over habit and effectiveness over efficiency. "
>
> ~ *Chris Fussell*

Leaders are intentional and clear about the purpose of what they are doing. Take a few minutes this week to become very clear about the purpose of a meeting you have, communicate that purpose effectively to those attending and maintain focus on that purpose. How efficient can you make that meeting?

Leadership In Action

ENTHUSIASM AND INSPIRATION

Leadership In Action

> " Leaders must exemplify integrity and earn the trust of their teams through their everyday actions. When you do this, you set high standards for everyone at your company. And when you do so with positive energy and enthusiasm for shared goals and purpose, you can deeply connect with your team and customers. "
>
> ~ *Marillyn Hewson*

Enthusiasm is infectious. When you are positive and enthusiastic about the shared goals of your team, the enthusiasm spreads and helps you connect deeply with others. Ask yourself this week, "What am I excited about that I need to share with my team so they can be excited too?"

> " A mediocre idea that generates enthusiasm will go further than a great idea that inspires no one. "
>
> ~ Mary Kay Ash

It is amazing sometimes how far some silly ideas spread when there is excitement for that product or service. Think about the pet rock - without enthusiasm, it is just a rock, but with enthusiasm, it becomes a pet. Enthusiasm is the key to its popularity. What idea would you like to expand with your staff, clients, or prospects? What is one thing you can do this week to spread enthusiasm for that idea?

Leadership In Action

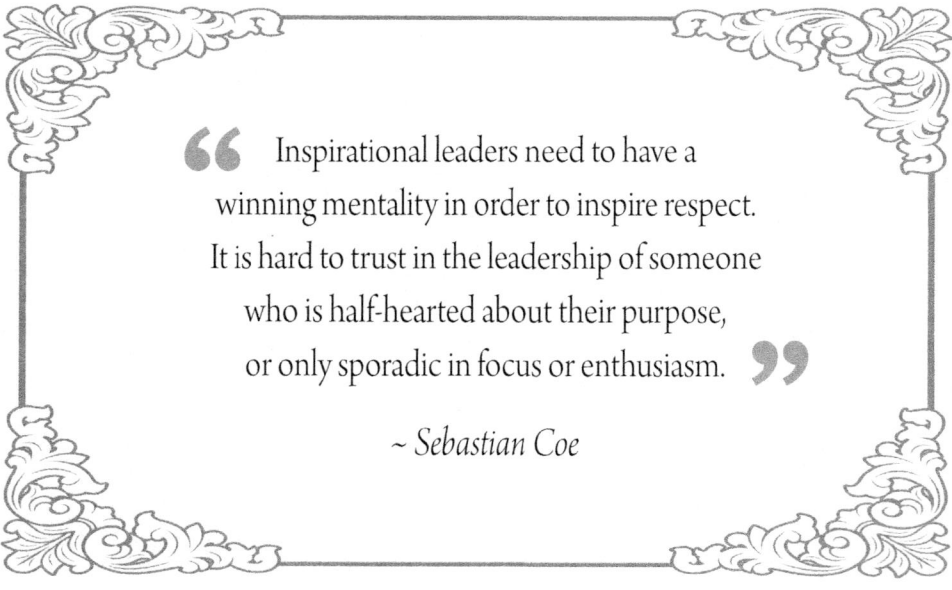

> " Inspirational leaders need to have a winning mentality in order to inspire respect. It is hard to trust in the leadership of someone who is half-hearted about their purpose, or only sporadic in focus or enthusiasm. "
>
> ~ *Sebastian Coe*

Commitment and enthusiasm for your purpose are necessary to get others to commit as well. And conversely, a lack of enthusiasm on your part will engender a lack of enthusiasm from your team. Does your team know your purpose? What are you doing to communicate your commitment and enthusiasm to them?

Enthusiasm and Inspiration

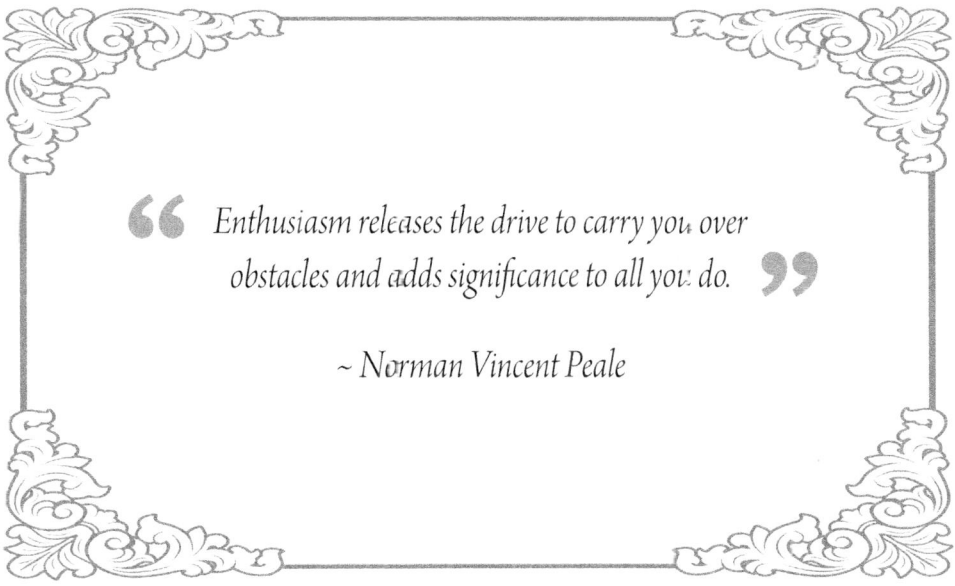

> *Enthusiasm releases the drive to carry you over obstacles and adds significance to all you do.*
>
> ~ Norman Vincent Peale

There are always obstacles and as a leader, you must help your team to move beyond those obstacles. One of the tools you can use is enthusiasm for the outcome! You and your team will find it easier to work through obstacles when you show enthusiasm.

Leadership In Action

> " I know of no single formula for success. But over the years I have observed that some attributes of leadership are universal and are often about finding ways of encouraging people to combine their efforts, their talents, their insights, their enthusiasm, and their inspiration to work together. "
>
> ~ *Queen Elizabeth II*

Leaders often think about how to combine efforts, talents, and insights with their team. Do you also consider how to consciously combine their enthusiasm? Enthusiasm is a multiplier for team efforts. What is one thing you could do to combine the enthusiasm of your team members and multiply their efforts?

Enthusiasm and Inspiration

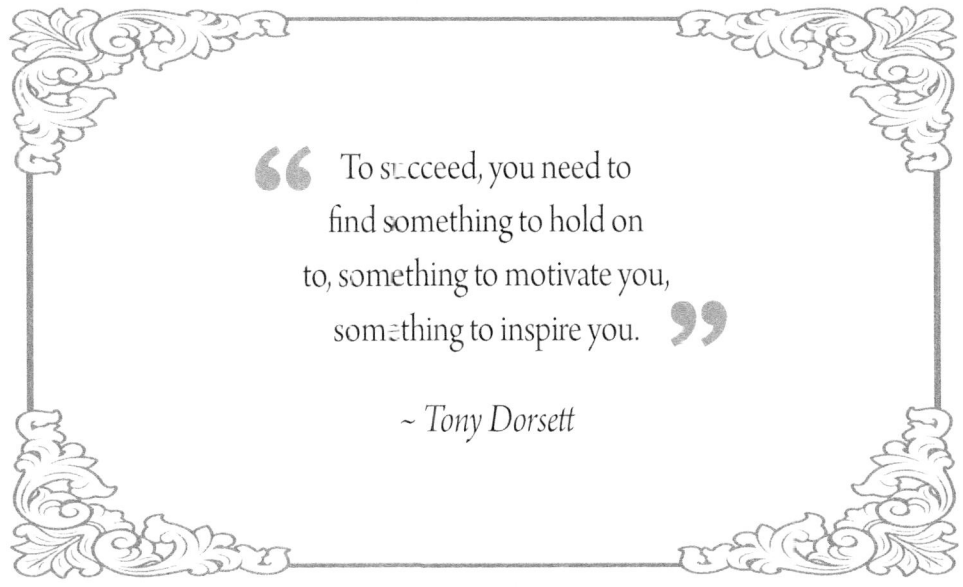

> "To succeed, you need to find something to hold on to, something to motivate you, something to inspire you."
>
> ~ *Tony Dorsett*

Whether you lead your own business or lead a corporate team, finding something to inspire you will keep you and your team going when things get difficult. What inspires you and motivates you to continue doing your best each day?

Leadership In Action

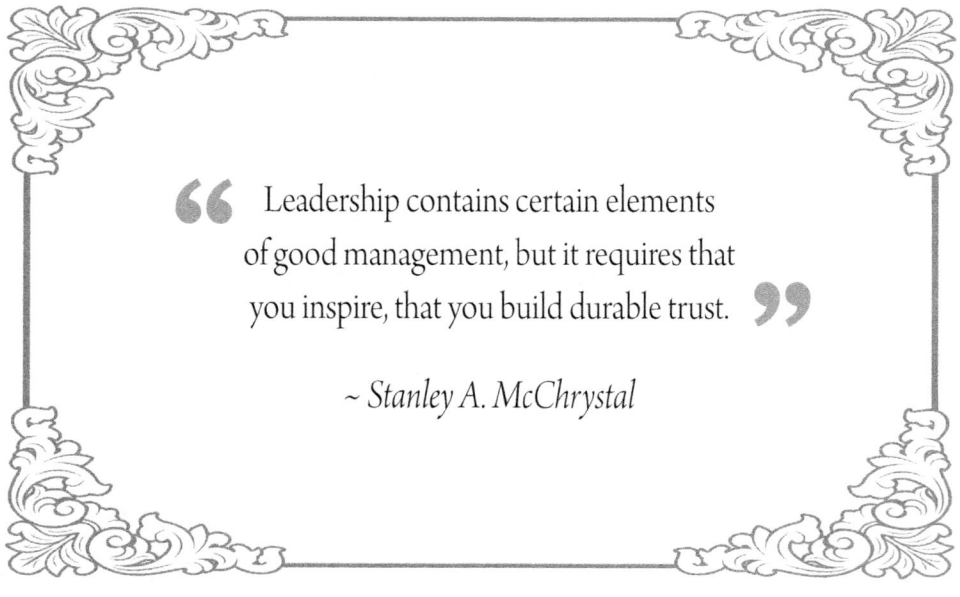

> " Leadership contains certain elements of good management, but it requires that you inspire, that you build durable trust. "
>
> *~ Stanley A. McChrystal*

Leaders work hard to build lasting trust with their teams. People are excited by the energy of inspiration, they get involved, they take action, and they want to be a part of what is happening. Inspiring your team is just one part of building lasting trust, it makes developing that trust faster and easier because the team is excited and involved.

> " There's no need to be perfect to inspire others. Let people get inspired by how you deal with your imperfections. "
>
> ~ Zaid K. Abdelnour

Leading is connecting authentically with others. Showing your imperfections makes you more authentic, people can relate to imperfect. Let them watch how you handle yourself in difficult situations and be inspired, it can build trust and connection as well as inspire them to handle their own imperfections.

■ ABOUT THE AUTHOR

A leadership book that turns inspiration into intentional action

A certified professional coach, group facilitator and change-maker, Lynne Roe helps entrepreneurs, business and non-profit leaders, develop a foundation of leadership that serves as a catalyst for growth. Applying knowledge and skills acquired over decades of working with small and large companies, and non-profits, she guides business owners and non-profit leaders in strategic planning, sound decision-making, leveraging the strengths of individual team members, and developing communications that build collaboration, respect, and trust. She provides clients with the tools to become outstanding leaders focused on transforming their organization for the future and serving as a positive force in their communities.

Lynne and her husband live in Northern New Jersey. Being an outdoor enthusiast, she loves to travel to beautiful locations and enjoy the scenery while biking, boating, skiing or hiking.

Printed in Great Britain
by Amazon

60618632R00074